From My Treasure Chest

FROM MY TREASURE CHEST

by

FLORA LARSSON

Salvationist Publishing and Supplies, Ltd
117-121 Judd Street, London WC1H 9NN

© The Salvation Army 1981
First published 1981
ISBN 0 85412 378 4

MRS COMMISSIONER FLORA LARSSON (R)
was born in Buenos Aires of a British father and a Swedish mother, Salvation Army missionaries in Argentina. She came with them to England before she was one year old and her childhood years were spent in various towns—and schools—around the country. With her Swedish husband, Commissioner Sture Larsson, she served as an officer of The Salvation Army in England, France, Norway, Sweden, Finland, Denmark, Chile and Argentina. Since being widowed in 1974, she has given more time to writing. She is the author of:

Viking Warrior
Just a Moment, Lord!
My Best Men are Women
Between You and Me, Lord
Towards You, Lord

Mrs Larsson's books have been translated into five European languages.

Printed in Great Britain by The Campfield Press, St Albans

Contents

Chapter   *page*

Preface
1 Just add water   1
2 How to live with ourselves—and with others   7
3 Intrepid travellers   13
4 The grace of humour   15
5 Where's your conscience?   19
6 The wonder of bridges   23
7 A pinch of salt   25
8 Needles and thread   29
9 Body and soul   31
10 Taste and see   35
11 You need an apron   37
12 Time enough!   41
13 Along Paris boulevards   47
    Lavender
    Perfume at a price
    At the post office
    The free shirt
14 From my heart to yours   53
    Melodies from the beyond
    The empty nest
    Facing widowhood
    Confessions of a grandma
15 Life's basic needs   61
16 The Mercy Seat   65
17 Hold your tongue!   67
18 Lost car keys   71
19 God's resources   73
20 What shall I wear?   79
21 Quicksands   83

Chapter		page
22	The growing pains of sainthood	85
	Saints abounding	
	Are we growing spiritually?	
	Wanted—spiritual cosmonauts	
23	Home-made bread	93
24	Is peace possible?	99
25	Mottoes	103
26	High days and holy days	105
	Christmas—the coming of a Babe	
	Good Friday—the festooned cross	
	Easter—remember!	
	Harvest—a packet of seeds	
27	My grandmother	111
28	Grow old with grace	113

Poems and prayers

	page
A word of appreciation	ix
Thank You, Lord	6
Queen for a day	14
Have it Your own way, Lord	18
I am a Christian	24
Righteous wrath	30
A wind in the tree-tops	36
The stars we kindled here	40
A light in heaven's window	46
I thank thee, son of mine	52
Hunger	60
God speaks in many ways	66
Shortages	72
Awkward saints	78
Too small a saint	84
Believe and receive	92
God of the open spaces	98
God who counts the stars	104
What counts?	112

Preface

In this book I am inviting readers to rummage with me among the items in my treasure chest, which is really just an old, battered trunk, worn in world wanderings.

You won't think it all treasure! I shall chuckle over some of the things I have gathered across the years as valuable souvenirs, which now seem almost worthless. Together we shall laugh at the old photos showing quaint dresses and hats, a few daring youthful frills, and say: 'Did we really look like that then?'

A few packets of yellowed letters tied with ribbon I put silently aside, but show you the colourful programmes of bygone events, great hits at the time, but which probably no one remembers.

Here are old things and new; longings, hopes, half-formed projects, good intentions—all mixed up. Sit beside me as I pick up my so-called treasures one by one and I'll tell you their story while we sip a cup of tea together. I am grateful for your company.

Flora Larsson

A word of appreciation

LUCINDA made a lovely cake
   As light as cake could be,
And with much pardonable pride
   She brought it in for tea.
Corinda said, 'Good gracious, Lou'
   A *currant* cake again!
You know I don't care much for fruit,
   I wish you'd made it plain.'

Lucinda sighed and then did say
How very dull she found the day.

Corinda made an apple pie,
   As nice as pie could be,
And though Lucinda wasn't thrilled
   She didn't let her see
But spoke in cheerful, kindly way,
   'My! but your pie's a treat!
Whene'er you don your cooking garb
   There's something good to eat.'

Corinda smiled and all that day
The sun shone gaily on her way.

1

Just add water

WE women have an easy time with our household duties compared with what our grandmothers experienced.

I think back to my own youth. I can remember life without electricity in the home, without radio or television, without washing-machine or refrigerator. We older people know how hard our mothers and grandmothers had to work at their daily tasks for the family. I stand 100 per cent for the lightening of as many household tasks as possible . . . but *sometimes I am afraid!* Afraid that we women are becoming so spoiled that we are in danger of losing our initiative, our joy of creation.

Women of the past had to be full of initiative. They themselves had to produce many of those things which we buy at the nearest shop. They were not in a quandary when the store was shut. With simple home ingredients they prepared what was necessary.

Look at old photographs and it comes almost as a shock to see the long, wide dresses with many small buttons—and just as many buttonholes, of course. All frocks were adorned with pleats and tucks and lace. Today we think we are clever if we can run up— with the help of an electric sewing-machine—a short, straight tunic which we have bought ready cut-out to our own size.

Don't misunderstand me. I am not pleading for a return to the so-called 'good old days' . . . for long hours of exhausting labour, for heavy voluminous clothing. The time for that is, I hope, for ever past. Though when I see some modern youngsters with lengthy skirts flapping round their ankles, I wonder whether the wheel of fashion has made a complete turn.

The terrible paradox of our times is that as we make life easier, less demanding, so do we weaken our inward strength, our tough core of courage and endurance. Some people think they are roughing it when they turn their electric blankets down to low heat!

But what do we women do with the time that we save? With the many hours that ready-prepared foods, so-called convenience foods, grant us, do we use the time saved in the right way? Of course, one time-consuming task is opening modern packaging. I find my fingers unable to manage some of the cellophane wrapping, so I bring my kitchen scissors into play.

It was a ready-mix packet of cake powder which set my thoughts whirling in this direction. In large letters I read the words: *just add water*. Yes, so far have we come, we modern women. Open the packet, pour the contents into a bowl, *just add water,* and pop it into the oven for half-an-hour. Then we can set on the table a cake which it would have taken our mothers a couple of hours to prepare and bake. That is a real triumph—not for us but for the factory which produced it. Some manufacturers, fearing lest we should see through their attempt to make us mindless robots, go one step further to make us feel that we are creative. On those packets we read: just add water *and an egg*. The sheer adventure, the excitement, the thrill of cracking an egg to add must surely make us feel like pioneers of olden days.

Perhaps some readers spurn ready-mixes and insist on preparing everything themselves. I admire their spirit! But the demands of modern life send many mothers of families out to work and the only way to provide meals on time is to take short-cuts and profit by half-prepared foods. Our mothers had more to do but they were generally in the home all day.

After a few years of using ready-mixes, I wonder if any woman could remain a clever housewife. We lose those abilities which we do not use regularly,. whether it concerns brains or muscles. Is there not a danger that we will lose our initiative and adaptability and that we become simply just-add-water women?

History is rich with the heroic deeds which women have performed despite great difficulties. While serving in Chile, South America, I met a woman who had had quite an adventure in her youth. Together with her husband she crossed the Andes mountain range from Argentina into Chile. I have made that same journey by train up into the snow line, but Mrs Pearson and her husband had to do it on mule-back. They had nine-month-old twins, which they held on cushions in front of their saddles. The journey over the mountains—in hot sun by day and biting cold at night—should have taken 10 days, but after the first few days the husband fell sick with typhoid fever. The family found an abandoned hut on the mountain-side and there they stayed for several weeks, with Mrs Pearson looking after her husband and the twin boys. Small groups of travellers or roving Indians came past now and again and from them she bought food, sometimes milk, and occasionally an animal that had been shot. Otherwise they would have died of starvation.

One must admire such a woman! She had grown up under hard conditions which had made her courageous and full of initiative. How would it have gone for her and her family if she had been a just-add-water woman?

Can you do mental arithmetic? That used to be something we practised at school, but I have not heard of it for a long time. Like most other women I shop in a supermarket where one pays for goods as one leaves. It is easy for the cashier to tot up the items on her adding-machine and tell the customer the total. But the other day I was in a post office where I asked for five 12p stamps. To my amazement the girl gravely pressed her calculator five times for the sum of 12p and told me I owed 60p. I had already worked that out for myself in my own little mind!

In another shop I bought two items from a salesgirl and when I offered her the money she said: 'Wait a minute. I have to work out the total.' She laboriously wrote down the figures and made it exactly what I had said. As I paid she offered the explanation: 'You see, I'm an art student. I don't know much about figures.'

This was in such contrast to something my husband and I saw when we visited Leningrad, Russia, a few years ago. I was enthralled to see how the Russian cashiers managed their job. They used frames with rows of 10 coloured beads such as my children played with when they were young. I had never realized how much arithmetic an abacus could perform. With graceful fingers the Russian women moved the beads forward and backwards along the various rows with surprising swiftness, and in a few seconds could announce the total. I admired them tremendously for their great ability. They used their brains and their fingers, plus a simple basic article.

Dear friends, where are we going? You might say to me: 'But life

3

isn't easy for me. I have lots of problems and difficulties and I don't have all the modern helps I should like to have.' I believe you, for there is no life without tension and strain, problems and sorrows, in these days.

The comparative ease of home life in our times must not lead us into becoming helpless 'watery' women. We must retain our courage and our resourcefulness, those great powers of the soul that grow only under pressure and necessity. And the daily burden of duties must not rob us of our privilege of making some contribution towards the well-being of others.

We have only to look around us or to read the newspapers to realize what a lot of trouble and sorrow has to be borne. Perhaps we can help to lighten someone's load; there may be some sick person that we can visit or write to, some lonely old person whom we can cheer, some baby-sitting we can do to allow a young couple an evening out, or to free a single parent for a few hours.

However busy we are, we should each find a way of *giving a little of ourselves* to lift another's burden. Not necessarily money, but time, thought, sympathy and prayer. This will enrich our own life. It is good that we Christian women know the way to reach the heart of God through prayer, to ask for His help and to receive His guidance, even while the hands are busy at many tasks.

Above all I feel that we should launch out into the search for a deeper spiritual life, a greater knowledge of God. In bygone days one had to dress and go out to be present at a meeting or church service, but now we can be served spiritual food through radio or television while we sit comfortably at home, quite possibly relaxing in a dressing-gown. All this abundance of spiritual and mental food, served to us on a tray as it were, can make us spiritually lazy.

Do we read the Bible for ourselves? Have we found out how to meet our own spiritual hunger through the word of God and through prayer? Is there some *adventure* in our spiritual seeking, or is it just a custom or duty?

You see, our spiritual experience is a very personal thing. There is no just-add-water religion which we can stack on our shelves and take down for use as we desire. For any religion to be a vital, living experience there must be seeking after God, the open heart, the listening ear for His voice. No one can mediate peace of heart through knowledge of God to us; we must ourselves accept it by an act of faith.

Sometimes we are satisfied with so little of God, so little of His grace, His guidance, His love. We stand like children paddling in the shallow water, while before us stretches the ocean of God's abundant provision.

O may God create in us a longing for more of Him, a desire to know Him in a deeper, more real, more effective way. Let us dare to go forward on our spiritual pilgrimage in faith, let us ask Him to use us to bless and help those around us.

We don't want to be watery women . . . we don't want to be watery Christians. We want to be alive in God's love, vibrant with His presence, conscious of His power.

In the New Testament we have some words which are a good antidote to the just-add-water mentality. They are found in 2 Peter 1:5-8.

'. . . add to your faith virtue; and to your virtue knowledge; and to knowledge temperance; and to temperance patience; and to patience godliness; and to godliness brotherly [sisterly] kindness; and to brotherly kindness charity. For if these things *be in you, and abound,* . . . ye shall neither be barren nor unfruitful in the knowledge of our Lord Jesus Christ.'

This is a glorious text! A wonderful and challenging programme for soul development. May we each aim to make it true in our own life.

Thank You, Lord

THANK You, Lord, for all Your goodness
    through the years of yesterday;
Thank You, too, for present mercies
    and Your blessing on my way.
Thank You for each revelation,
    thanks for what You choose to hide;
Thank You, Lord, for grace sustaining
    as I in Your love abide.

Thank You, Lord, for sunlit pathways,
    Thank You, too, for byways rough.
Thank You for the fruitful summers,
    also for the winters tough.
Thank You, Lord, for fragrant flowers
    growing right amid the weeds,
Thank You for the peace You give me
    even while my spirit bleeds.

Thank You, Lord, for wayside roses,
    even for the thorns beside,
Thank You for the prayers You answered
    and for those that You denied.
Thank You, Lord, for precious comfort
    in my hours of grief and pain;
Thank You for Your gracious promise . . .
    life eternal I shall gain.

Swedish text: August Storm
Translation: F. L.

2

How to live with ourselves—and with others

WE are ourselves and different from every other person in the world. Each of us has two eyes, a nose and a mouth, yet think how many variations there are upon that simple, monotonous theme.

Our fingerprints are unique to us and therefore a valuable basis for identification. In South American lands it is customary to carry an identity card on which the owner's thumb-prints are shown. When a foreigner registers with the police for a permit of residence, prints are usually taken of all 10 digits. It is no easy matter to get the black ink off the fingers afterwards, as I know by personal experience.

It is now also possible to make a voice analysis recording the inflexions, intonations and speed and thereby build up a diagram of that person's speaking pattern by which identity can be established.

Millions of cells in our bodies carry our own personal genetic code. Each of us is a new combination of all possibilities, differing from all others.

Many people long to be someone else. They hate themselves with an open or hidden hatred. 'If only I were so-and-so I could find a way out of my problems. . . .' Years ago I saw a comic cartoon of a doctor saying to his patient: 'This is a very serious case of allergy. You are allergic against yourself!'

If we don't get on with ourselves, matters are indeed serious. I remember learning by heart a verse which commenced:

> *I have to live with myself and so*
> *I want to be nice for myself to know.*

Yes, we need to be 'nice' so that we can live in harmony with ourselves. It is said that as we get older we don't get better or worse, but only more like ourselves.

We need to accept ourselves physically. We are a mixture of lots of varying blends. Mother's eyes, father's hair, Aunt Edith's jutting chin, grandpa's broad forehead, grandma's long, tapering fingers . . . there is no end to our inheritance, much of it that we cannot trace.

But each is a new edition—a mixed-up but updated issue supremely original. People come in various shapes and sizes—long and short, thin or fat (shall we say generously proportioned?), fair or dark, lightly or heavily built. And here comes a strange truth: nearly every one wants to be different from what they are. Those with straight hair long to be naturally curly but have to use the hairdresser's skill to achieve that end. Those with square faces try to imagine how wonderful it would be to have a delicate oval shape. Most people are troubled about their nose. After all, it is central, or should be. They imagine it to be too short or long, too broad or narrow, too snub or aquiline. Even those who resort to plastic surgery to improve their nose are not always happy with the result. We need not worry if someone appears to be eyeing our nose critically. They are hardly thinking about us at all but merely wishing their mouth was smaller, like ours.

We are as we are! The best thing then is to accept our physical form and concentrate on doing what can be done to make it look its best. Good posture has a lot more to do with how clothes appear than many people think. Straight back, stomach in, head up, weight controlled—these all help to make the most of what nature has given us.

Now let us consider our *temperament*. That too is largely what we have inherited from our forbears. Some people are lively and quick while others are phlegmatic; some are naturally a bit hot-tempered while others are placid and even, seldom upset. Some people are born optimists while others tend to pessimism. And then there are inherited traits. Away back there in our past is some old Aunt Maria who didn't like spiders, or spinach, or 'spuds', and we find this same dislike embedded in our make-up.

Our temperament, though, is not always at the same level. It swings up and down according to the weather, our health, circumstances and food intake. Some people are like living

8

barometers, registering in their moods the falling or rising pressure. We all are part of nature which has its own rhythmic seasons and times: winter and summer, night and day, growth and decay, ebb and flood.

We need to adapt ourselves to what we are, realizing our strengths and weaknesses, our potentials and drawbacks, natural gifts or their absence. We must be realists and try to see ourselves objectively. If we are colour-blind, we don't enrol for an art course. If we have no ear for music, then singing is not for us. Aim high but not too high. When we admit to ourselves that certain gifts and graces are not for us, decide at the same time what our strong points are. If we are not musical we can, perhaps, declaim, recite or join a drama group. If we feel too nervous to take a public part we can try to learn to write, and one learns to write by writing. It is as simple as that. We must compensate for what we lack by branching out in another direction.

In the centre of Santiago, the capital of Chile, there is a rocky mount called Santa Lucia, around which traffic has to diverge. A massive though not high mountain is not the most enviable thing to have in a modern city. One proposal was to dynamite it and carry the rubble away, but that would have been a long and very expensive project. Instead it was decided to make it into a tourist attraction, a natural scenic viewpoint. By making roads on the lesser gradients, cutting steps in the rock in some places, building out terraces from which the magnificent panorama of the Andes mountains could be seen, and adding flower beds, what started out as a minus in the city became a big plus. That is what we must seek to do: change our minus to a plus by skilfully developing what is possible for each of us and ceasing to hanker after what is beyond our power.

Finally, *aim at self-development.* We are living material. We have not been poured into a mould in which we have stiffened so that there can never be any progress. We can change ourselves, improve ourselves, with patience and practice. We can develop a harmonious personality. That is what we must aim at—inner harmony instead of strife. In order to like ourselves we must be able to respect ourselves. We must not allow ourselves in acts or habits which we know are wrong, so that we carry a bad conscience around within us. That alone will inhibit our freedom of expression and create nervous tension.

Above all, seek God's help. When we ask for His aid it does not follow that He will wave a magic wand and transform us on the spot to small angels with a halo and fluttering wings. We remain ourselves but our *best* selves! The traits of our character are not basically altered but with God's help and guidance we develop our inward resources. And we learn to live at peace with ourselves.

Having achieved inward harmony we must learn to live with others around us. It would be easy to avoid strained relationships if we lived alone on a desert island but we are all part of 'the madding crowd'.

The frequency of separation and divorce in these days highlights the great difficulty that arises when folk attempt to live together. Two people in love with each other, who have chosen to marry, can reach the stage where they can't bear the sight of each other.

When we lived in Finland a friend told us that he and some business associates had been shocked by the number of marriage breakdowns occurring and being reported daily. After some deliberation they decided to see what they could do to save a few of the marital catastrophies. Their plan was to put an advertisement in the daily paper reading: 'If you are planning divorce and have children, ring first to number. . . .' The members of the group took it in turn to man the telephone and for four days and nights the calls came through in quick succession. These Christian friends did their best to reason with the parties concerned, making a special plea on account of the children involved, but they felt they had little success so they reluctantly gave up their project.

It is not only in marriage that difficulties occur. Within the family living together under one roof, or between friends sharing accommodation or workmates on the same job, there can easily arise great storms from small causes.

These troubles originate in the fact that we are all different and all see matters from our own viewpoint. In an art class I attended a woman sat to pose as a model in the centre of our circle. She had a placid, aged face and she sat with great patience while we tried to sketch her. There were about 20 of us but no two sketches were alike, though we had all copied the same subject. Some had her face in profile, some full-faced and others sketched her from the back. We each depicted her as we saw her, from *our* angle. All working on the same project had produced differing results.

When people live or work together it is always best to have clearly defined duties or spheres of involvement. In an emergency one can offer to help out with extra tasks, but generally speaking it is best that each one knows where the dividing line lies.

One's rights is a ticklish subject. We humans like to defend our territorial rights and boundaries just as do animals and birds. To know one's own rights and to respect other people's is the basic principle on which to work, with the good intention of seeking a compromise when trouble seems brewing. One can give a point to win a point.

Personal taste is another area where we differ greatly. We must not try to make over someone else to our ideas of how things should be done. Even a simple matter like boiling an egg can lead to conflict! One prefers to pop the egg into boiling water; another says start it off cold and bring it to the boil, which is quicker and therefore cheaper. Breakfast table rows can start over the egg or the toast or newspaper and cast a lengthening shadow over the whole day.

To live harmoniously with others does not only mean avoiding quarrelling, but it implies bringing something to the relationship; a good-humoured reaction to problems, a helpful hand when needed, and a kindly word of appreciation or encouragement as often as possible.

Each person is enclosed within the private door of personality. How shall we come into contact unless we have a key? May I suggest three keys that we could try?

The first is a smile. It is said that we use fewer muscles to smile than to frown. And we look much better too! A smile beautifies the face more quickly and cheaply than the most renowned cosmetics. Look at ourselves in the mirror with frowning face and surly mien, then whisk on a smile and note the difference. Immediately we look several years younger and much prettier! So try to smile at others as often as we can during the day.

The second key I suggest is an appreciative word. There is usually something which can be praised. If a friend appears in an ugly green frock, we can remark on the unusual neck-line or the graceful way the pleats fall in the skirt. We can say 'thank you' more often and in a pleasanter voice for the small services rendered to us in the course of the day. Why should we be mean about words of appreciation when they cost nothing more than the effort of saying them? And with what warmth they fall into another heart!

The third key is a friendly action. It can be a telephone call, a cheery letter, a bunch of flowers from the garden, a visit or simply a handwave across the road.

If we use these three keys we shall find they open the way into other hearts and lives, and as we learn to know people better we shall understand them more readily and accept them as they are.

There is an old French legend about an aged saintly man, much loved in the quiet village where he lived. One night he was visited by an angel who said: 'God has noted your life of gentle helpfulness and He wants to give you a gift. What do you choose?'

The old man thought for a moment and then he replied: 'I want to be of blessing and help to others without ever knowing of it myself.' (You need to be a saint to ask for such a gift, instead of money, power or influence.) He continued his quiet walks along the village roads, chatting with the peasants at their work, calling on the sick, smiling at the children, and wherever he went people felt uplifted, as though a weight had been taken from their hearts, the sick began to recover, children ceased quarrelling and laughed joyously. The old man had received his gift from God.

No angel will visit us tonight as we sleep, asking us what gift we would choose, and yet I know that each of us in our heart wants just what the old saint asked for: to be able to bring some sunshine and help into other lives which we touch in daily life. May that be our experience, even if we never learn of it from the grateful recipients.

3

Intrepid travellers

ONE of my secret wishes was to see the *Kon-Tiki*, the balsa raft on which Thor Heyerdahl made his epic voyage from Peru to Tahiti, and with our appointment to Norway in 1969 my wish became fulfilled. It was a thrilling moment for me to stand beside the frail craft on which six men crossed the Pacific, relying solely on sea currents and wind, trusting their lives to bundles of reeds lashed together with plaited reed ropes.

Nearby in a museum was housed the *Fram* (meaning Forward), the ship on which Nansen made his famous journey in search of the North Pole. After sailing as far northwards as possible, he moored the *Fram* to an ice-floe for 20 months, allowing the ship to drift with the sea currents. Not coming near enough to the Pole, Nansen and a companion, Johansen, began a lonely 15-month overland march through snow and ice but they were unable to reach the Pole. They returned alive after suffering untold privations.

The spirit of man! What it will not endure to prove a theory or make a conquest. In 1969 we had the moon landing to thrill us and the biggest wonder of all is that for this space adventure, the astronauts were in constant contact with their base in Houston, and we could watch the descent to the moon's surface on television.

Nansen disappeared for three years and no one knew whether he was still alive. Heyerdahl and his crew had a radio and could send messages to ships, but the astronauts were in *constant contact* with ground control, to receive guidance and reassurance. Isn't this a picture of how God treats us who are finding that 'to follow Christ is the greatest adventure in life'! We can have constant contact with Him through prayer, and possibly our greatest need is a deeper sensitivity to His voice, a sturdier reliance on His guidance and a firm faith in His ultimate plan working for our good.

Queen for a day . . .
—a mother's plea

GIVE me one day, a single day,
When you strew roses on my way;
From morn to eve just pamper me
And fuss me to the nth degree.

Just for one day let me be queen,
Then afterwards with pleasant mien
And gratitude for what has been,
I'll go back to the old routine:

The stalest crust, the spotty egg,
The chair which limps on broken leg,
The roughest towel and patchiest sheet,
The blanket too short for my feet. . . .

The much-cracked cup, the burnt-up toast,
The gristly portion of the roast,
The blunted knife, the boniest chop
That ever left a butcher's shop. . . .

The greenest plum I'll choose to take
Nor blink my eye at crumbly cake,
At melting choc or sticky sweet . . .
Whate'er is second best I'll eat.

Why! I prefer the boniest fish,
The smallest apple on the dish;
The hardest pear you e'er did see
Is just the very one for me.

But for one day, on Mother's Day,
Let me the role of Home Queen play
With loyal subjects hovering by,
My every wish to satisfy.

4

The grace of humour

THERE is nothing like good, clean humour to relieve the tensions of mind, soul and body. A hearty laugh will open dammed-up channels through which the sparkling, clear waters of common sense and a balanced judgement can flow. Salvationists are a fun-loving folk. In fact, Bramwell Booth wrote: 'I have sometimes dared to think that humour was one of the special graces of salvationism.'

Honest, homely humour is the spice of life. Blessed is that home or office which can daily count on the bubbling exuberance of sanctified humour from one of its number. We are not all born humorists, but for one who can make a joke there are always nine who can appreciate it. Humour oils the wheels of duty. Humour spreads a delightful fragrance down the dry and dusty roads of routine. It creates oases in the desert of monotony. Under its gentle and delicious ministry our stiffened muscles and strained minds relax and, in new-found pliancy, find also a solution to baffling problems. As an angel of light, humour stands with flaming sword between us and despair.

There is so much pressure in life, so much effort demanded of us that, if we have not recourse to the brief relaxations that a sense of humour provides, we are in danger of breaking.

> *God, give me laughter as a buckler,*
> *Lest to the blows of life I yield;*
> *When my head is bowed to press of foemen,*
> *Lord, give me laughter as a shield.*

Humour will help to keep us sane through the stresses caused by conflicting personalities around us. It will relieve us when we feel 'dully mad at everybody and acutely so at some'; and, hand on heart, which of us is a complete stranger to that experience?

A sense of humour will help us in our dealings with others. It is often the window through which spiritual light can stream. Blessed is that one who can use it wisely. In his book on the 23rd Psalm, Dr John McNeill tells the following story:

> I remember a big stalwart Novocastrian coming in to me in the vestry after I had preached. He was certainly far through. 'Oh, Mr McNeill,' he said, 'I'm so miserable. I feel so dead. I'm no Christian. I never was truly converted. I'm only a hypocrite.' And he fairly groaned in his misery. 'Oh, I feel so dead. . . .'
> 'Man,' I said, 'if you were taking your last look now at all that's mortal of a dear friend before the lid was screwed down, how would you feel if your friend should suddenly stretch himself in his coffin and groan out, "Oh, I feel so dead"? When a dead man says he's dead, he's never so dead as he says he is!'
> I'll never forget how he laughed, and the darkness went off his big strong face like the mists lifting off Ben Cruachan.

A redeeming sense of humour will prevent us from taking ourselves too seriously, will prevent us from using an over-sensitive conscience to torture ourselves over small shortcomings. Confessed and forgiven they must be but never magnified to great mountains of iniquity and dwelt upon until they become brakes on our spiritual progress.

> *Once in a saintly passion,*
> *I cried in desperate grief:*
> *O Lord, my heart is full of guile,*
> *Of sinners I am chief.*
>
> *Then stooped my guardian angel*
> *And whispered from behind:*
> *Vanity, my little man,*
> *You're nothing of the kind.*

(Thomson)

We cannot claim to have any real sense of humour unless we can laugh at ourselves. A particular weakness of us older folk is that a solemn seriousness regarding our own importance possesses us. We cannot magnify ourselves without the risk of getting other people out of focus and certainly not without the danger of our projected importance being bumped into by passers-by who do not realize how much space we need to manoeuvre in. May God give us the grace to keep a twinkle in our eye.

And where shall we find our humour? Why, all around us. In the little happenings of every day, the bright, shining, glad moments, the gloomy irritations, the sudden surprises, the anti-climaxes, the dull patches; all, all are grist to our mill if we will but take them and transmute them by the alchemy of a happy spirit which looks for the shaft of light piercing between the dark clouds.

If all else fails us, visit a zoo. The Creator who made giraffes and kangaroos quite definitely revealed a sense of humour, and each time I see those animals I enjoy the joke with Him. If there is no zoo near us, try a duck-pond. F. W. Harvey writes:

> *From troubles of this world*
> *I turn to ducks,*
> *Beautiful, comical things . . .*
> *When God had finished the stars and the whirl*
> *of coloured suns*
> *He turned His mind from big things*
> *to fashion little ones:*
> *Beautiful tiny things (like daisies)*
> *He made, and then*
> *He made the comical ones, in case*
> *the minds of men*
> *should stiffen and become*
> *dull, humourless and glum:*
> *And so forgetful of their Maker be*
> *as to take themselves . . .*
> *quite seriously.*

In advocating the cultivation of a sense of humour I make a strong stand against flippancy. God forbid that its contaminating hand should touch the ark of our sacred things. C. S. Lewis, in *The Screwtape Letters,* states that 'the habit of flippancy builds up around a man the finest armour-plating against God that I know. It is a thousand miles away from joy; it deadens, instead of sharpening the intellect.'

Solomon assures us that 'a merry heart doeth good like a medicine' (Proverbs 17:22). Cultivate, then, gaiety of spirit and 'put a cheerful courage on'. When our soul has finished its deepest pleadings before the Lord perhaps it would not be out of place to add this verse, part of a prayer found in Chester Cathedral:

> *Give me a sense of humour, Lord,*
> *Give me the grace to see a joke:*
> *To get some happiness from life*
> *And pass it on to other folk.*

Have it Your own way, Lord

HAVE it Your own way, Lord,
  You've won!
I lay my weapons down.
You would not give me blow for blow,
  no steel met mine,
And yet I am as vanquished.

Your only weapon was invisible . . .
  'Twas love!
  Love?
What might has love?
'Tis but a feeling, a soft-hearted
  sentiment.
What power has love to conquer
  the spirit's strong defiance?

I know not, cannot know.
I only felt my efforts feebler grow;
The sword slipped from my slackening grasp
  and shattered lay the shield of my self-will.
  You've won!
Have it Your own way, Lord.

5

Where's your conscience?

THE games mistress in one of my schools was a stickler for discipline and order. Only a small deviation from duty would bring her before the group with flashing eyes and the inevitable question: 'Girls, where's your conscience?' None of us knew the answer but we all understood what she meant.

People come in many different varieties but all have something in common—a conscience. All consciences are not alike. Some people allow themselves to speak or act in a way that would be unthinkable for others. While the conscience is not the voice of God within us— there are too many shades of conscience for that to be possible—it is a voice *for* God and right in our hearts. Someone has rather cynically said that a good conscience is another name for a bad memory. Without agreeing with that it is certainly true that everyone knows what it feels like to have a guilty conscience over something we have said or done.

We know its nagging pressure, its dominant voice over all other sounds around us, its insistence on being heard by constant repetition. We can turn off the radio and television, refuse to answer the telephone or receive callers, yet conscience will sit on our shoulder, shouting in our ears that which we hate to hear yet must acknowledge as true. It is said that conscience makes cowards of us all. When all around us might be applauding us with a 'Bravo!', conscience is cur enough to inject a stabbing 'Hypocrite!' and we know that we have been inwardly found out and unmasked, even while our face smiles in acknowledgement of popular acclaim.

Conscience has been called the still small voice that makes you feel still smaller, but perhaps the best description came from a young Indian lad. When asked if he knew what his conscience was, he replied: 'My conscience is a little three-cornered thing in my heart that stands still when I am good but when I am bad it turns round and the corners hurt a lot. But if I keep on doing wrong, by and by the corners wear off and it doesn't hurt any more.'

And there we have what is known as a hardened conscience that 'doesn't hurt any more'.

Some people have an over-sensitive conscience. They are troubled about small details in no way connected with moral right or wrong, but are simply the result of training in childhood by super-scrupulous parents following a narrow code of conduct. When adult we have to weigh what we allow ourselves in the light of our own standards.

Charles Dickens, who so admirably dissected the intricacies of human reasoning and conduct, has an amusing paragraph about conscience in *The Old Curiosity Shop:* 'In the majority of cases conscience is an elastic and very flexible article, which will bear a deal of stretching and adapt itself to a great variety of circumstances. Some people, by prudent management and leaving it off piece by piece, like a flannel waistcoat in warm weather, even contrive in time to dispense with it altogether; but there be others who can assume the garment and throw it off at pleasure. This, being the most convenient method, is the one most in vogue.'

At what age does conscience awake in a child? Thinking back over my own life, one memory stands out clearly when conscience spoke so loudly that I have never forgotten it. I suppose I was about three years old at the time.

Looking back I see myself hiding behind the curtains in the front room. From whom am I hiding? From my sister and brothers. And why? Because I have something in my hand which is good to eat and I don't want to share it. What can it be that I am so secretive about? Surely at least a lovely apple or a box of chocolates!

No! Nothing so fine as that. Just a few small sweets that I had bought for a farthing which somebody gave me. Not wanting to share my tiny treasures, I swallowed them hastily, and young as I was I can still recall two feelings which filled my heart, two thoughts which impressed my childish mind.

The first was that sweets don't taste so nice eaten quickly like this, all the time listening hard to hear if anyone was coming.

Secondly, when I had swallowed the sweets I felt so ashamed of myself because I had been greedy. It's not nice to hear the voice of conscience saying, 'You greedy little girl!', even when one is but three years old. If I had shared with the others there would not have been more than one sweet each, but I should have enjoyed that one better and saved myself a lifetime memory of being a greedy little pig.

Every year conscience money is sent to the tax office, British Rail and other such bodies from people who have failed to pay what they owed yet have found it difficult to live with the burden on their mind. One woman, it was reported, had written to the taxman anonymously explaining: 'A few years back I made a false tax return. Since then I don't sleep so well at nights, so I send £50 herewith. If I still find I can't sleep I might send a bit more later. . . .'

A good deal of trouble is sometimes caused by fanatics, people with a twisted conscience, who follow an evil course in the firm belief that they are doing right. One classic instance of that occurred in 1415 in the dawn of the Reformation, when the martyr John Huss of Bohemia was burnt to death as a heretic. The wooden pyre had been prepared and Huss was led out to be bound to the stake when he noticed a poor old woman hurrying forward with a few dry sticks to add to the firewood.

'Woman, have I ever harmed you?' asked Huss. 'No,' was the reply, 'but you are a heretic. I have only a little firewood to last me the whole winter, but I gladly offer these sticks to help remove an enemy of God from the earth.'

The Apostle Paul, before he met Christ on the Damascus Way, was a fierce antagonist of the believers in Jesus Christ. He had them arrested and thrown into prison, thinking he was doing God a service. He was a typical example of the unenlightened conscience. But after the Damascus Way experience all his zeal and energy were thrown into the opposite direction—to the preaching of our Lord and His resurrection from the dead.

In the account of his many adventures for God recorded in the Acts of the Apostles we read that Paul stated one of his life principles to be: 'I . . . train myself to keep at all times a clear conscience before God and man' (Acts 24:16, *NEB*). A clear conscience! Before God . . . and man! What a high ideal that is. It will give us peace within and poise as we face the heavy demands of each day. It will be the basis of serenity of heart and mind, granting us an inward strength. A clear conscience is not simply the result of forgetting our misdemeanours. Rather it is calling them to mind and seeking forgiveness, where possible making restitution.

It is never easy to go to someone and say, 'I'm sorry!' That little act of reparation can prevent many small quarrels from escalating into family feuds. And what a wonderful feeling of release and relief floods the heart when we have made amends.

The doctor said 'twas nerves, although I knew
Another reason for my tired limbs
And why I couldn't eat or even sleep . . .
I'd had a tiff with Mary Ann—and how
The sting remained of those hard words I'd said.

I went to Mary Ann and made it up;
She was a dear and gave me such a hug,
It cheered my soul. Now I'm as right as rain,
And doctor's tonic has gone down the drain.

And a clear conscience before God—is that possible? Yes, it is gloriously possible! A deep sense of the forgiveness of sin through the love and mercy of God is one of the most hallowed and uplifting experiences in life—the nagging of conscience stilled, the burden of guilt lifted—our hand placed firmly in God's hand as we face the future with Him.

'I train myself . . .', said Paul. A clear conscience is not a once-for-all-time attainment. It is a question of maintaining a right relationship and living as we believe God would have us live, each day seeking His guidance and strength; keeping short accounts with Him by yielding ourselves afresh to Him each morning and closing each day with a prayer to Him.

6

The wonder of bridges

IN her autobiography Rita Snowden gives a fascinating glimpse of how she watched from her window the gradual building of the great bridge over Sydney harbour. She told how the two sections, commenced simultaneously from opposite sides, gradually grew towards each other in a graceful arch. Finally the actual date and time of the dramatic joining was predicted. The appointed day dawned, rivets were driven in the last steel girders, and the sections fitted perfectly. A triumph of engineering skill, enabling heavy traffic to thunder across the bridge daily.

Bridges—the wonder of them! Not only those built of steel and concrete, but those bridging the gulf between nations, between races, between social classes and individuals. Would that as much planning, time and energy went into completing such projects.

But the greatest bridge which has ever been brought into existence does not span a gulf between two lands or two nations. It is the spiritual bridge which makes possible the approach of sinful man to a holy God.

During the three years of Christ's ministry on this earth, the bridge between God and man grew longer and stronger and one day, nearly 2,000 years ago, in a tragic act on a low hill outside Jerusalem, the last span was added and the bridge was completed. Christ's words from the Cross were: 'It is finished' (John 19:30)! And Paul said: 'God was in Christ, reconciling the world unto himself' (2 Corinthians 5:19). The dying thief was the first to cross. Since that day millions have ventured by faith across the Bridge of Reconciliation and found pardon and peace with God through the merits of Jesus Christ.

I am a Christian

I AM a Christian and ever will be
    Till sun and moon all their course have run.
I am a Christian! In that I glory
    Although the worldlings at me poke fun.
I am a Christian and will remain one,
    I love the Saviour for He is mine;
To Him I render my deepest homage
    For He is worth it, my Lord divine.

I am a Christian! O grace abounding!
    My Jesus saved me from slavery;
I'm called a Christian by those who scorn me
    Yet persecution still leaves me free.
I am a Christian! To fight I'm ready,
    The Christian's armour and sword I claim;
I go to battle for Christ my Saviour,
    To win great vict'ries in His dear name.

I am a Christian! On earth a stranger,
    No race can claim me, no land is mine.
All earthly joys seem so cold and empty
    For in my heart burns a fire divine.
I am a Christian! My rightful Homeland
    Lies o'er the frontiers of sin and need;
There in my Homeland no good thing's lacking,
    Instead of crumbs there's a feast indeed.

I am a Christian! O how it comforts
    In times of sorrow, like music sweet;
It lifts my soul up on eagle pinions
    To hover high o'er the world's deceit.
I am a Christian and if death's fingers
    On my heart's door knock with ghastly knell,
I'll fear no evil for Thou art with me,
    My Jesus saves me and all is well.

J. Grytzell
Translation from Swedish by F. L.

7

A pinch of salt

WHAT is our best friend in the kitchen? A sharp knife? A pair of scissors? A measuring cup? No, I think our best friend is a packet of salt. A schoolboy definition of salt was 'that which makes potatoes nasty if you don't put any in'.

Have you ever stopped to ask yourself what salt is? Man quarries it, collects it, refines it, packets it and sells it, but the salt itself is a gift to us from God, a part of His creation.

Salt is a combination of two elements, sodium and chlorine. Sodium alone is violent and burning and could do great damage. Chlorine by itself is a powerful gas, yet united these two elements form common salt. There are two kinds of salt: sea-salt, thrown up by the tides and dried by the sun, and rock-salt, found in deposits in the earth.

The greatest known deposit of salt in the world is in the Dead Sea area, but the most famous salt mines are in Wieliczka in Poland. They have been worked since the 13th century. These salt deposits cover an area of many square miles, and about 65 miles of streets and galleries have been tunnelled in the salt. Electric trains carry hundreds of workers between solid walls of rock-salt, the crystals of which glitter like gems in the light of electric lamps. Workers in this underground city of salt are proud to show visitors the Cathedral of St Anthony which was carved from salt in the 17th century. Its walls are adorned with carved statues, sparkling as though studded with gems when light catches the facets of the crystals.

Some salt is necessary for health. In hot and humid climates where one perspires freely, salt tablets are often advised, to replace the lost salt. We know by experience that when we perspire a lot and a drop of perspiration touches our lips, it tastes very salty. In

Central Africa children love to lick pieces of salt as our children lick lollipops. It is a great treat for them. Also in Africa the fairy story of Hansel and Gretel is changed so that the little house they find in the forest is not made of gingerbread but of *salt,* which is much more of a delicacy there.

Late in 1956, when European events seemed to point to the possibility of atomic war, a rumour spread wildly round Paris that salt was a protection against radioactivity. In the space of two or three days all salt in the shops was bought up by anxious housewives. Some even went so far as to sprinkle it on their heads! In wartime in some lands salt has been rationed in addition to the usual bread, fat and meat.

The word salary comes from the word salt. The Roman soldier who served in hot countries was given a ration of salt or money to buy it, this being called his 'salarium', or salt money. From this derives our present word for payment for services rendered.

A man who did not do his duty was said to be 'not worth his salt'—a saying which persists to this day.

Of course, in some illnesses the doctor recommends a saltless diet which can be very trying to follow. I myself had three months once on such a diet and oh! how tired I was of the insipid taste of potatoes and rice boiled without salt. The best solution is to eat as much raw food as possible with the natural salts contained in them.

Salt stimulates flavour but it must never call attention to itself. If it does, too much has been used.

Salt preserves. We housewives all know salt fish and salt meat, preserved in brine. We are in the era of frozen foods but in olden days salting down food was the only way known. Salt in the final rinsing water 'sets' colours after dyeing.

Salt disinfects and in weak solution can be used for gargling or bathing eyes.

There are many customs relating to salt. One generally known is that it is considered bad luck to spill salt and to avoid trouble one should throw a pinch of salt over the left shoulder. One summer I was privileged to visit Italy and to see Leonardo da Vinci's great painting of the Last Supper on the wall of the Santa Maria delle

Gracie Church in Florence. Among the 12 apostles round the table, Judas can easily be picked out, as he has knocked over the salt-cellar.

In the East an invitation to a meal is couched in the terms 'Will you come and eat salt with me?' and friendship is spoken of as 'There is salt between us.'

In the past it was the custom in certain continental countries to deprive a prisoner of salt as a punishment. Now it is the doctors who deprive their patients of salt, not to punish but to cure them!

In feudal days when the lord and lady of the castle dined in the great hall with the lesser gentry, a large salt-cellar separated them. The nobility was said to sit 'above the salt' and the commoners 'below the salt'.

One still takes 'with a grain of salt' a statement hardly likely to be true.

* * * * *

As recorded in Matthew 5:13, Jesus said to His disciples: 'Ye are the salt of the earth.' The merging of two elements makes natural salt and in the same way the union of the divine and human makes Christians. We cannot pull ourselves up to God by our shoe-laces. God has stooped to us and stretched out His hand of forgiveness. It is for us to accept His pardon and to become His children, to love and follow Him. Our conversion can never be the result of our good desires or good works. It is always an act of God, through grace.

Just as salt stimulates the flavour of a dish, so religion adds zest and interest to life. We who believe in God should be happy people. We have our problems, our trials, our temptations, but we have a hidden source of inward strength, peace of heart, quietude of mind.

Too much salt spoils a dish and our religion must never make us awkward to live with. Some religious people are like the Pharisees, making stern laws both for themselves and for other people, law rather than grace. The Christian life is a life of joy and liberty and every single person who becomes converted to Christ should be easier to live with.

27

The presence of a Christian in any company should be a good influence. How important it is that the mother of a family should be a Christian woman. Into her hands is given the supreme task of moulding growing lives, of training and developing young souls. It is not an easy task! It demands all we can give in effort. And yet some women try to do it without God's help.

You are the salt in your home, in your family, in your district, among your acquaintances. God has placed you there because He has a task for you to do. You must hold up standards of purity, honesty, truth and caring love. There is sin all around us in the world today. Open sin, hidden sin, sins of the body, sins of the mind. God calls us women to bring the healing and antiseptic influence of good lives into our surroundings—to be as salt in a corrupt environment.

Christ also gave His disciples a warning: 'If salt becomes tasteless, how is its saltness to be restored?' (Matthew 5:13, *NEB*). Wonderful and useful as salt is, it can lose its saltiness and be fit for nothing but to be thrown out. This is a solemn thought. What is it that causes the loss of the precious savour? It is exposure to impurities or damp. Once gone, the saltiness never returns.

This, however, is not true of a Christian who has lost her spiritual savour, her trust, her sparkle as a child of God. The analogy with salt breaks down, for the wonder of Christ's love is that He is ever ready to reaccept us into fellowship. If a Christian has lost contact with Christ through carelessness, prayerlessness or actual sin, he or she can be restored by the grace and mercy of God. Oh what a wonderful gospel of redeeming love it is our privilege to proclaim!

For anyone who maintains an outward form of religion but who has lost the radiancy of their Christian faith, whose heart is cold and seemingly dead, this message is for you: God can again meet with your soul, restoring lost joys of fellowship, pardoning the past, giving strength for today and hope for the future. Will you let Him do it for you? Your part is simply to invite Him to return to your heart and life. He will do the rest.

8

Needles and thread

WHAT did women do before the age of needles and thread? I can imagine how they hunted out some sharp bone or porcupine quill and with great labour made a hole in the end. Then a search began for grasses which were strong and flexible enough to act as thread. I think back to Adam and Eve in the Garden of Eden. We read in Genesis 3:7 that 'they sewed fig leaves together, and made themselves aprons'. I wonder what they used!

Away in the interior of Peru is a tribe of primitive Indians. A home league member in Lima, the capital, heard that the women of the tribe were without needles and sewing cotton. Collecting from friends and fellow-leaguers she was soon able to send off a parcel containing 600 needles with large eyes (such as the Indians prefer) and 150 large reels of strong thread. With the parcel went a warm greeting from the home league members.

Three months later came a notice from Lima post office that a large parcel awaited collection by The Salvation Army. What could it possibly be? A mystified home league member staggered home with a huge bundle sewn up in gaily woven cloth. When she opened it, out fell about 300 tiny packets containing rice, beans, sugar, maize, wheat, and all kinds of native flours and dried berries that she did not know by name. With tears in her eyes she realized that the native women who had received the needles and thread had each tried to say 'thank you' by sending a small gift out of her meagre household store. The tiny individual packets became almost sacred symbols from one woman's heart to another.

Righteous wrath

MASTER, it is not fair, I said,
that I should feel as though I had done wrong.
   I had to speak!
Your honour was at stake and I
      who love Your Name
felt my blood boil with righteous wrath
      and indignation.
Hot and fast the words poured
      from my lips
as I upheld Your cause.

*   *   *

I looked into Your face
to catch Your glad approval of my zeal;
      but my glance fell
before the quiet censure of Your eyes.

9

Body and soul

WE humans have a dual nature. We belong to two spheres—the physical and the spiritual. We are body *and* soul. The one mortal and doomed to perish; the other immortal, destined for eternity.

It is no wonder that we are more conscious of our body than of our soul. The body talks loudly for itself, whining. 'I'm hungry, thirsty, tired, aching. . . .' The soul's voice is quieter but nevertheless it can distinctly be heard at times as the voice of conscience, or of moral judgement, or simply the conviction that one course is right and the other wrong.

To be able to live with this duality we must be wise. Our aim should be to have a healthy soul in a healthy body, although that might sound idealistic.

We all know that we have good days and bad days, and middling days which are neither the one nor the other but just plain ordinary and monotonous. If only we could be at the top of our form every day! It would make life easier if we jumped out of bed each morning feeling confident and energetic, eager to tackle the duties ahead. So often the start of the day is heavy and dull, with a mountain of tasks peering threateningly over our shoulder as we drink our morning tea.

It is of interest to know that scientists have been studying our biological rhythms, those cycles of changing patterns in health, emotions and intellect. We are not always at our peak . . . in fact we are at times very far down. But the further we are down the nearer we are in time to the moment when we go up again. That is comforting to know! These cycles of change are of different duration and when we happen to be at the lowest ebb on all biorhythms at one and the same time we are indeed in trouble. It is at such moments that there are accidents in the home or at work, quarrels, loss of temper, and the first steps are taken towards divorce. An oft-repeated word of advice is: 'Never get out of the train in a tunnel.' Never take an important decision when you are down.

Surely there is also a spiritual cycle of ups and downs, of ebb and flow; times when the heart feels hard and cold and other moments when we are warmly responsive to God.

How are we to run a straight race and hold the right course between these physical and emotional changes? Our goal must be clear before us and to that end we must fulfil our obligations, do our duty and complete our tasks, with or without pleasant feelings.

In an examination one of the students finished early and, handing his paper to the invigilator, remarked: 'I can't do any better than that as I'm not feeling quite well today.' The professor accepted the brief attempt, fixed the student with a penetrating gaze and said: 'Learn this, young man. Half the work of the world is being done every day by people who are not feeling quite well.'

Body and soul need to be good friends, for they have an intimate relationship. They are united by many unseen ties. The body's health affects the soul. The soul's well-being is reflected in brighter eyes and good temper. My body is not my enemy nor should it be my master, but rather my tool which serves me in the way that I require. Paul expressed it beautifully to the Corinthians: 'Do you not know that your body is a shrine of the indwelling Holy Spirit, and the Spirit is God's gift to you?' (1 Corinthians 6:19, *NEB*).

A shrine of the Holy Spirit—what a lovely phrase. To think my body is that! I must look after my body then, not pampering or neglecting it but giving it the attention and care it needs to keep it in the best possible working condition.

In my young days Fay Inchfawn was a popular writer and poet who with her strong Christian faith must have influenced great numbers for God. In her 'Psalm of Hope for the Body' she writes:

Thou art more than a clod;
More than a rough-spun dress;
More than a sheltering pod
For a soul's homelessness.

More than a fettered slave
Bound to a master;
Destined to fill a grave,
Born to disaster.

Thou art a thought of God;
A long-planned implement
Designed to fill His hand
And made for His content.

It is well known that Francis of Assisi called his body Brother Ass and at times maltreated it badly in his search for holiness of life. If his food tasted especially good he sprinkled ashes on it to make it more difficult to eat. Whatever his poor stomach and intestines thought of that punishment I do not know, but it certainly was not treating his body as a shrine for the Spirit of God. He welcomed lice in his clothes, regarding them as God's instruments to aid his growth in humility, and at times his followers must without his knowledge have killed these 'heavenly pearls' as Francis called them. This was, of course, the outcome of the religious teaching of that period which insisted that the body was evil and must be treated harshly.

Of Suso, another saint, it was recorded that he did not wash himself for 25 years to discipline his body (and also surely the folk around him!). It is said that one could sense his soul's purity by one look at his dirty face. What a good thing that we have passed beyond such beliefs!

To keep body and soul working in harmony a certain self-discipline is required, above and beyond the other pressures that our life imposes. The outer rules are the demands of our work or studies, our home duties and necessary social contacts. The self-discipline concerns mainly our free moments—not many of them perhaps in the course of a day—and our acceptance of certain norms of living.

For our soul a daily time of prayer and meditation is as necessary as food for the body. The swift upreaching of the mind towards God; a grateful 'Thank You, Lord' at any time when things go well; a 'Help me now, Master' when difficulties arise. These only take seconds yet they keep the lifeline open between the soul and God. Choose some time at morning, midday or evening for a few minutes of more leisurely prayer and meditation over a text from the Bible, and of remembrance before God of those we love. Sitting in a bus or train, walking the street, one can be in contact with the heavenly Father. Such moments are precious, strengthening the soul and confirming our faith.

Bodily discipline is necessary to keep us in the best possible health. This includes a sensible programme of eating, working, sleeping and exercise. Most people eat too much and exercise too little, with the result that they are 'heavy' in more ways than one. We must learn what foods agree with us and what is best avoided, and keep to the diet that suits us best as far as we can. A supper of cheese and pickled onions is liable to give nightmares to all but the stoutest stomachs. Know that if we eat salt herring even the grace of God won't keep us from thirst. We may have to refuse a dish that our taste-buds approve of, or take very little of it if we are in company, simply because experience has taught us that it causes indigestion and thereby lessens our fitness.

There should also be some intellectual discipline, some new learning or skill that we acquire. This can come from a book or magazine or through a television programme. Even in these days of pocket calculators it is useful to do a little mental arithmetic at times to keep the brain in working condition.

Finally, remember that a true religious belief helps the functioning of both body and soul. Fear and anxiety are some of the greatest causes of ill health. Another enemy to heart-peace is the bearing of grudges and resentments against another person or against our circumstances in life. Our faith in God and in His caring love can throw up a parapet of defence against the attacks of bitterness, envy or spite to which we might be tempted.

Any inner conflict reduces our ability to think and work. It makes us feel tired without any physical reason. Tension or nervousness—a feeling that we cannot cope—minimizes our possibilities. Sometimes we try too hard to succeed.

Dr Stanley Jones tells of a new Indian stenographer that he engaged. He was so anxious to do well that he pressed his pencil so hard on the paper that the table shook. The missionary watched his efforts for some moments then said: 'You'll never be a good stenographer while you try so hard! Relax! Let your pencil glide easily over the paper.' The young man laughed and his tension disappeared.

Body and soul must combine to create a happy, fulfilled life, and that is certainly worth having and worth working for.

10

Taste and see

NOT far from where we lived in Oslo, Norway, a new supermarket opened and it was advertising all sorts of good things at reasonable prices with *free tastes* of many delicacies. On a cold morning, through deep snow, I trudged with my shopping trolley—taking it more as a support against a fall on the icy roads than to bring home heavy packages—towards the brilliantly lighted store.

Shivering as I entered the warm premises I was immediately offered a taste of hot cauliflower soup. A stand a little farther on gave me a minute portion of sausage and mashed potato. Feeling quite pleased with myself I made a few purchases, then noticed a queue at another stand and got tinned fruit and cream. It looked as though my lunch had been taken care of, but I did long for a cup of coffee.

My shopping finished I turned homewards intending to take my hot drink on arrival. Calling in at the nearby local shop, what did my gladdened eyes see but a row of small coffee cups with an invitation to taste the newest blend. So I got my coffee after all!

It is obvious that shop-keepers are not offering free tastes of so much without hoping to make sales of their products. They know the magic of a tasty mouthful on a cold morning, and I don't doubt that their sales mounted. To be convinced of the goodness of a new brand, people had to be induced to take the first step, a single taste. Then, with appetite awakened, they would want more.

It is no wonder that the psalmist presses us to 'Taste and see that the Lord is good' (Psalm 34:8). If people will only stretch out their hands in desire towards God, make a first contact with Him, then their spiritual appetites will grow until their need is met.

A wind in the tree-tops

THERE'S a wind in the tree-tops, I hear it a-blowing
Awake to the coming of spring!
There's a budding and stirring, a greenness of growing,
Awake to the coming of spring!
Refreshed is my spirit anew, my heart tells me just what to do:
I throw on my coat and I go, out there where God's fingerprints
    show.

There's a song in my soul and its message I capture:
'Be glad in the Lord and rejoice!'
There's a gayness and lightness, a wonderful rapture,
'Be glad in the Lord and rejoice!'
Refreshed is my spirit anew, my heart tells me just what to do:
I lift up my voice and I sing, Christ Jesus is Saviour and King.

There's a voice in my ear and I hear it repeating:
'Behold I am with you alway!'
This assurance brings courage, all weakness defeating,
'Behold I am with you alway!'
Refreshed is my spirit anew, my heart tells me just what to do:
I fall on my knees and I pray: Lord, bless me and use me today.

11

You need an apron

APRONS are very useful things, and most of us made our first acquaintance with them as children. They have two very good points. They can protect a clean dress or hide a dirty one. Aprons usually mean work. No one puts one on when going to bed! In the morning on goes the overall ready for the day's work.

When I became a cadet, to be trained as a Salvation Army officer, three kinds of apron were required by the outfit list for the training college. A white one for serving at table, a coarse one for scrubbing and some coloured ones for ordinary housework. The white one I never used in the college, never being entrusted with the task of serving visitors at table, and years afterwards I gave it away, still unused. The other kinds got their fair share of wear. I found it particularly hard to have to don the coarse apron to scrub out other cadets' cubicles for a half-hour immediately following midday dinner.

It was the fashion when I was a teenager to embroider small silky afternoon tea aprons. They were bought with the pattern—usually of raised roses—stamped on to them, and it was a simple matter to choose the colours and finish the design. Such pinafores were not for service but for show. The most fanciful were not much bigger than a handkerchief, surrounded by lace.

The former Minister Lagercrantz of Sweden in one of his books described a visit to Lady Buxton's mansion in England. There it was the custom every morning for all the servants to come to the big hall for daily prayers. When the bell rang the head servants appeared, followed by the lower servants and lastly the stable-boys and kitchen-maids. And the strange thing was that the highest rank of servant wore the tiniest apron. She was the housekeeper, and over her black silk frock she had fastened the smallest, thinnest piece of white muslin and lace that you can imagine. Her apron was definitely an indication of her high estate, far above any coarse servitude. Following her came servants with gradually larger and plainer pinafores and finally the little kitchen-maid with a great sacking apron reaching down to her feet. How she must have looked with awe at the housekeeper and longed for the day when she, too, could throw off the large, coarse apron and have the right to wear a dainty bit of muslin and lace.

Should one be ashamed of being seen in an apron? Certainly not! Work is honourable and to be suitably clad for it is sensible.

Jesus said: 'I am among you as he that serveth' (Luke 22:27), and He certainly gave us a good example. I am sure that He must have worn some kind of apron when He worked in the carpenter's shop in Nazareth before the years of His public ministry. Then do you remember the incident when He washed the disciples' feet? We find it in John 13:4, 5:

'He riseth from supper, and laid aside his garments; and took a towel, and girded himself. After that he poureth water into a basin, and began to wash the disciples' feet, and to wipe them with the towel.'

There was no apron handy, so He took the towel as a substitute. Our Lord and Master knelt before each one of His disciples and performed the lowly task that usually a slave or servant did. What an example He gave us! An example of willing, loving, humble service. May we all learn that lesson from our Lord.

Peter in his epistle mentions another apron. Moffatt's translation of 1 Peter 5:5 reads: 'You must all put on the apron of humility to serve one another.'

The apron of humility! Do you think that apron is a few inches of silk and lace? No! I think it is a great big overall kind of pinafore, in which you can do the roughest sort of work. Have we got this 'apron of humility in service' among our other clothes? We have at home all shapes and sizes of aprons and overalls, some for house, the garden, the workshop, our job. Some are new, some old and patched, some threadbare. Some are big, some are small and some are just dainty trifles given us as gifts. But somewhere we all ought to have this apron that Peter writes of, 'the apron of humility to serve one another'. Every day we should be looking for chances to help and cheer some other soul.

May God make us wearers of the apron of humility and, in a spirit of love and friendship, may we try each day to serve our fellowmen and to lighten the burden on another's shoulders by some little kindly service.

The stars we kindled here

WE often sing of faith's reward in glory,
A crown awaiting in the heavenly sphere;
But in that crown no other stars will glitter
Than those we kindled in our lifetime here.

Those stars are sorrows that we changed to gladness,
They are the help we gave when need was great;
The lamps we lit amid the gloomy shadows,
The tears we dried for one disconsolate.

They are each noble cause we fought for bravely,
Each soul we won, each vict'ry in His name,
What we for Jesus' sake have suffered gladly,
Each sacrifice, each fear we overcame.

The brightest star of all we wear in heaven
Will be the good that we by stealth have done.
The kindly deed that no one saw but Jesus
Will then shine clearer than the noonday sun.

When at God's throne we lay our life's endeavours,
All will be tested, judged at its real worth;
But in our diadem no stars will sparkle
Except those stars we kindled here on earth.

In Norwegian by H. A. Tandberg
Translation: F. L.

12

Time enough!

CHILDREN have a very strange idea of the passage of time. I remember that when I was a child there seemed to be an immense desert of time between the oases of Christmases. Nowadays it seems to me that I hardly put away the festive decorations from one Christmas before I have to take them out for the next.

During the Second World War we lived in Sweden, which was neutral. Our neighbour, Finland, was engaged in deadly warfare with Russia, a country many times its size. Swedish families were asked to adopt Finnish children temporarily so as to save them from the bombings. We took a boy of eight years old into our home and he quickly settled down as one of the family. My son John was about six at the time and the lads became firm friends.

One day I was telling stories to the boys and having run out of the more conventional kind of tale I began to describe the rigours of the Stone Age. How thousands and thousands of years ago people lived in caves; how with flint knives they hunted and killed wild animals for food, then skinned them and wrapped the furs round themselves for clothing. The boys' eyes grew round with wonder and as I finished my story the Finnish boy asked breathlessly: 'Mamma, were *you* alive then?'

*   *   *   *   *

Time is the world's greatest treasure but it is also the most wasted commodity. We carefully hoard our coins of base metal and we throw away our golden hours.

In our daily allowance of time we are all equal. President, king, peasant, labourer, child—all receive the same portion of 24 hours a day, no more, no less. For some it is too much and they do not know what to do with it. For others it is too little. One thing hidden from our knowledge is for how long shall we continue to receive our 24 hours at a time? Are we among those people who are continually saying, 'I haven't got time'? I must plead guilty myself, for those words are often on my lips, but I would remind you—as I remind myself—that we each have all the time there is! No one is more favoured than another in that respect.

Time divides itself easily into past, present and future. We can think of it as a river and ourselves as children sitting on the bank, playing with our hands in the water as it passes us. That which has already passed we shall never see again—it has gone for ever. From a distant source in some unknown mountain flows the water which will reach us in the future. How much there is of it we do not know. But for *today* we can dabble our hands in the little portion of the great river of time which for a few hours touches our lives.

Or, to change the simile, time lies like a heap of golden hours stored in the heavenly bank. Each day we present our cheque and receive our 24 precious hours, to do with them as we please. It never occurs to us as we lay our heads on the pillow at night that in the morning there will be any difficulty in getting our new supply of time. But the day will come for each of us, sooner or later, when our reserve of days is exhausted and our account is closed.

I suppose that all of us possess a watch or clock, so that it is not difficult for us to follow the passage of time. Thousands of years ago the sun was man's time-keeper and its journey across the heavens was the only indication of the hour. Then the sun dial was introduced, followed by sand clocks, water clocks, and finally the clocks and watches we know today.

In various lands I have seen many interesting clocks. In Strasbourg, France, as a large clock strikes 12 noon a procession of figures representing the 12 apostles passes before Christ, bowing at His feet, while He makes the sign of the cross. During the solemn advance of these 12 figures a cock perches high on a turret, flaps its wings and crows three times. Other clocks I have seen play tunes at different hours. Though vastly different, these clocks have one thing in common. They register the inevitable and inexorable march of time, whether they do it silently or with music and action. *Time flies!* And the older we become the faster it appears to fly.

A refreshing story in these days of speed and bustle is told by a traveller just back from the Highlands of Scotland. His watch having stopped, he asked an old man the time. The ancient Highlander considered the question carefully then said: 'Now let me see . . . let me think. . . . Yes, this will be Friday afternoon, for I'm almost sure that yesterday was Thursday.' That was near enough for the old man but it would hardly be adequate for any of us.

Think what a lot of things we can do with time! We can *spend* time by using it to bring us profit; we can *take* time to do things properly and carefully; we can *husband* time to get the most possible out of our precious hours, and we can *serve* time in prison, although I hope none of us will have any experience of that nature. We can *gain* time by working rapidly; we can *waste* time by doing nothing at all, and we can *beat* time to music. We can *lose* time by being lazy and slow; we can *give* time to study; we can *save* time by learning to be methodical; we can *kill* time, and to kill, as we know, is a crime. We can also do what the Apostle Paul urges us to do: 'redeem . . . the time, because the days are evil' (Ephesians 5:16). What did he mean? He was advising Christians to use carefully every opportunity which the Lord gave them to witness for Him, to serve Him and do good to others.

What are we doing with *our* time? I hope we are using it well. Let us remind ourselves that our present physical body is time-bound. When our allotted measure of hours has run out, the machinery of our bodies will stop. Our portion of time will be exhausted and our account will be closed. But time itself will go on. . . .

A strange incident happened once to one of the official clock-winders of the Law Courts in London. He did nothing else but wind and adjust clocks, having 800 in his care. One day he was inspecting the works of a large clock 35 yards above street level when his clothing was caught in the machinery. The chiming of the clock drowned his cries for help. Hundreds of people passed to and fro in the street below, all unconscious of the drama being enacted above their heads, for the huge clock went on ticking as if nothing had happened. Some hours later two mechanics on a tour of inspection found the dying man caught up in the winding machinery, but the clock was still ticking remorselessly. Yes, we pass away, one by one, but time marches on.

Perhaps some of us remember the motto on the sundial in a Chinese garden. It has been much quoted, for it is very true: 'It is later than you think. . . .'

'Redeeming the time,' wrote Paul, 'because the days are evil.' Are not the days we live in evil, in like measure or even greater? In Paul's day there were no atomic or nuclear weapons threatening the destinies of mankind. One writer put it like this: 'We have the feeling that very soon now God will come down to earth and say to humanity the way they say it at the saloon bar every evening: "Gentlemen and ladies, it is closing time." '

But it is not the intention of the writer to scare anybody with fears of the future. We ought to consider the *present*. Recently, while reading a sacred song during my morning devotions I came across a line I do not remember seeing before and it stuck in my mind with a strangely comforting persistence. It was this: 'Time is still your friend.'

I have never thought of time as my friend. My master, yes, even at times my inexorable enemy, but my *friend,* no. We are accustomed to the thought of Father Time as an old man with flowing beard and with a scythe over his shoulder with which he cuts off lives as grass is cut. Can time be my friend? Yes, I believe it can! It can give me the chance of doing those things I know I ought to have done and yet which I have put off, for one reason or another. Today is ours, but tomorrow we cannot reckon with. Again I quote some words of Paul, this time in his second letter to the Corinthians (6:2): 'Now is the accepted time; behold, now is the day of salvation.'

Time is still our friend. What a challenging thought! Those who are as yet uncommitted still have a chance to kneel at the feet of Christ in surrender. Those who are called to some special service but who have been disobedient to the heavenly vision still have a chance to respond to the divine call. Those who have something on their conscience which has not yet been confessed and put right, either with God or man, 'time is still your friend'. For people who have been careless in their prayer life or whose heart has grown cold and hard, or whose faith has been dimmed on account of the difficulties of the Christian way, there is an opportunity to place their hand again in that of Christ.

Time is God's gift to us. How are we using it? Some day we will have to give account of it to God. Can the Lord count on our help in the great task of spreading the light of the gospel? May I ask that as these words are being read each of us bows her head, closes her eyes, and says to herself: 'Time is still my friend.' Then let us pray:

Lord God, I thank You that every day can be a new beginning. I come to You afresh with all my needs. Help me to redeem the time because the days are evil. May I walk in Your ways; may I do Your will; may I serve You faithfully and may I be ready when I hear Your call. Amen.

A light in heaven's window

THERE'S a light in heaven's window
   Kindled by a Saviour's hand,
There's a Father-heart awaiting
   Upon that far-off strand.
Through the maze of earthly windings
   Dare I hope to reach that land?

    There's a light in heaven's window,
    Softly shining from afar;
    When the gloom of night enfolds me,
    I see God's guiding star.

When at times the darkness deepens,
   Shade of selfishness and sin,
God's clear beacon of forgiveness
   Wakes hope again within.
Can a wayward, faulty mortal
   Life eternal ever win?

There's a light in heaven's window,
   Pledge of God's renewing grace;
This world's darkness cannot quench it,
   Its ray a path doth trace.
My heart burns with eager yearning,
   Shall I one day see His face?

13

Along Paris boulevards

Lavender

I SUPPOSE every girl in high school stands in awe of her head-mistress. I know I did. She was a tall and serene woman, walking the corridors with graceful carriage, and always leaving behind her a gentle wafting of lavender. I decided then and there that I would do the same when I grew up.

Great areas in the south of France are given over to the culture of lavender, which is grown in long rows about a foot broad. In between the rows the dry reddish-brown earth shows through. When the lavender is in bloom the effect is wonderful. The long straight rows of purple flowers contrast vividly with the reddish earth, all bathed in sunshine from a clear blue sky. We were fortunate to pass through the lavender district just when it was at its best. The sight and scent were unforgettable.

A little later, when walking along a crowded boulevard in Paris, I was struck by the strong and delightful scent of lavender around me. To my amusement I saw a diminutive donkey standing on the pavement with two little baskets, one on each side of his broad back. The baskets were filled with small packets of lavender and, as added propaganda, a man was spraying passers-by from a bottle of perfume. On its head the donkey wore a yellow straw hat with its ears poking up through holes in the brim, as is the custom in the south of France.

It really looked very quaint and attractive and many people bought packets of lavender. I could not help wondering what the donkey thought of the crowds hurrying past and whether he had got to the point of hating the smell of lavender. In the rush of hurrying humanity which always seems to fill the Paris boulevards, many would not have noticed the vendor of lavender had he not sprayed the air full of perfume. It was the waft of scent which first drew attention to his wares.

In 2 Corinthians 2:14 we read: 'God . . . uses us to reveal and spread abroad the fragrance of the knowledge of himself' *(NEB)*. Paul writes of the inner fragrance emanating from a life lived in communion with God. It is not a sprayed-on commodity; no money can buy it, no friend can make a present of it. It is God's gift, the result of the Holy Spirit living in the heart.

Modern perfumes are packed in most attractive ways, but it is not the beauty of the bottle which creates the perfume. It is the contents. The perfume would be identical even in a medicine bottle. In the same way the fragrance of Christ can be spread abroad by a very ordinary person who lives in daily contact with the Lord.

In *Ships of Pearl,* F.W. Boreham tells of a commercial traveller in a small English town who spent the morning in calling upon his clients, displaying his samples and soliciting orders. At midday he heard the prolonged sound of a siren. Shortly afterwards he detected a most delightful perfume. He glanced around, expecting to see some garden full of flowers, but there were only dusty old warehouses and offices.

Still sniffing the enchanting perfume, he met a man and asked him the secret of the fragrance. 'Why! didn't you hear the siren?' he was asked. 'That was the signal for the girls at the perfume factory to leave for lunch, and in hurrying down the street they carried the fragrance with them.'

The factory girls spread the fragrance unknowingly, because they had been in contact with it. In like manner, living in daily fellowship with our Lord, some of 'the fragrance of the knowledge of himself' will exude from our lives and be used to make Him known to others.

* * *

Perfume at a price

IT is fascinating to walk through the giant emporiums along the Paris boulevards and see the marvellous products offered for sale. One has to harden one's heart and keep a tight hold of the purse-strings. Almost the whole ground floor of each large shop is given over to the sale of perfume. It is thrilling to see the glitter and display of the myriad boxes and bottles and to smell the attractive scents.

A relative in the United States of America sent me some dollars and asked me to buy her a small bottle of 'Joy'—the world-famous perfume by Patou. I felt quite overpowered by this errand, which was outside my usual modest shopping expeditions. I summoned up my courage and asked the prices of the precious flasks. My dollars could purchase only a small phial and I packed it carefully and posted it.

Great was my dismay later to learn that the package had arrived, but the bottle was broken and the only 'Joy' that had arrived was a smell in the wrapping paper.

Having to accept that the fault was mine, I took my own money and bought another bottle of the expensive luxury. This time I made sure it was packed in many layers of cardboard and paper. All went well and the 'Joy' arrived safely and gave pleasure.

This incident reminded me forcibly of the words of Jesus in His last long talk to the disciples: 'No one shall rob you of your joy' (John 16:22 *NEB*). Of course, we can lose our joy in the Lord by carelessness or prayerlessness, but it is wonderful to have His word that no person and no circumstance can rob us of the joy of His presence in our lives.

* * *

At the post office

WAITING one day in a post office queue in Paris I overheard a long conversation between a young Arab woman and the official who repeated: 'But I can't write out the telegram for you. That is forbidden.' And the young woman answering with sobs: 'But I *can't* write. I have never learned.'

'Then go home', she was advised, 'and get someone who can write to fill in this form. Bring it back and we will send it.' The young woman cried in her despair so I offered to write the telegram for her. She was from Tunisia and had never gone to school. After filling in the address for her I asked her what was the message to be sent. 'Only this', she replied: 'Good news!'

Think of it! To have good news to send and not being able to do it. The telegram was soon dispatched and a happier Arab woman returned home.

God had a message for this world but it did not seem to grasp it, although He conveyed it by His chosen prophets. Finally, He sent His Son Jesus, and then the message became clear: it was *good news* from God, a way of salvation from sin, a new birth into spiritual life, and a Father-hand to clasp.

*   *   *

The free shirt

ONE day when we lived in Paris my schoolgirl daughter came home to tell me excitedly: 'They're giving away free shirts on Boulevard Haussmann. I asked for one but they said I was too young and that I ought to tell my mother to come.'

I laughed and told her there must be a catch in it somewhere. 'No,' she maintained, 'they said several times that they would give away free shirts to the first 10 who applied for them. Why don't you go there one day and try, Mamma?'

A few weeks later I was going along Boulevard Haussmann when I saw a crowd on the pavement and heard the word 'chemise', ie shirt. Remembering what my daughter had told me I approached to hear a woman say: 'I will give a free shirt to the first 10 to accept one of these cards.' I took a white card and waited to see what happened. Soon all 10 cards were disposed of and the crowd closed in to see what would transpire.

The saleswoman stood behind a pavement counter piled up with men's shirts in cellophane wrappings and she began to extol the wonderful qualities of the goods which her firm manufactured. If one was to believe what she said, they were the most marvellous shirts in the world.

'Now', said the woman, 'I am going to give a free shirt to each one who has accepted a white card. Each one can choose style and colour and size. What is your wish, Madame?' turning to one of our group holding the cards.

The size and desired colour being made known, the saleswoman produced two identical shirts, saying: 'Madame would like a free shirt of this type, and I will give it to her provided she buys a similar shirt of the same wonderful quality for . . . new francs,' and she named quite a high price.

The cat was out of the bag! Here was the secret. You could obtain a free shirt by buying another at more than its value. Several of the women accepted this 'bargain' and went home with 'two shirts for the price of one'. But I had certain misgivings about the quality of the material so I surrendered my white card without profiting by buying two shirts to surprise my husband with. And I have never regretted the decision I made to forego the offered free shirt.

One is sometimes caught by tricks of propaganda and by slick salesmanship, but I think it is a general rule all over the world that, however enticing the offer seems to be, however advantageous to the buyer, the seller never parts with his article at a loss. In other words, he is out for his own profit, not for philanthropic ends.

There is only one gift of value which can be described as *free*, and that is what Paul alludes to in his letter to the Romans (6:23): '. . . the gift of God is eternal life through Jesus Christ our Lord.' That is a free gift of eternal worth.

I thank thee, son of mine

FOR that sweet, rapturous joy of motherhood
When first thy downy head lay on my arm;
For deepened sense of need for heavenly grace,
That I might keep thy priceless soul from harm,
 I thank thee, son of mine.

For all thou gavest me through seven short years,
For ringing childish laugh and shining eyes;
For hugs and kisses and dear baby ways,
Thy need of me which made me mother-wise,
 I thank thee, son of mine.

For smiling face when weakness laid thee low,
For pain and sickness ever bravely borne;
And last . . .
For greater understanding of earth's woe,
For sense of kinship with all those who mourn,
 I thank thee, son of mine.

14

From my heart to yours

Melodies from the beyond
HEAVEN is filled with beautiful music! How do I know it?

I heard some of it once and with my whole being I long to hear it again. God granted me for a few moments a thinning of the veil between this life and the next. I did not see but I heard . . . and how I wish that others, too, could hear what I heard, for it is difficult to describe.

I will open my heart and reveal quite simply what happened.

My first-born, a lovely boy of seven years with blue eyes and fair wavy hair, lay dying of leukaemia. We, his parents, watched by his bedside all night long in our flat in Stockholm. In another room lay our tiny daughter, four weeks old, sleeping peacefully in her cot.

Death . . . life. . . . Why? A thousand whys!

It was over! Our last hope for our son's life had fled. He came to us from God. From our arms he returned to God's. Of that we were sure, but the parting was hard. The wound ached and bled in our heavy hearts.

I walked from my son's deathbed into the other room, picked my baby from her cradle and fed her. Blessed be duty when the heart sorrows!

Then I heard the music. Soft, delicate, like the quiet plucking of harp strings. I listened intently. It must be the radio, but no, that was not on. Perhaps the neighbour's wireless? I pressed my ear against the wall but no sound came from next door. I walked from one room to the other. Wherever I went the music accompanied me. Then the truth dawned. Those beautiful strains were in my mind. I was hearing them with my inner ear. It was no earthly music; it came from the Great Beyond. The melodies of heaven.

I sat down to listen with my whole being. There was no recognizable melody. There were no chords. Sweet, tender, soothing and joyful, the liquid notes followed one another like the rippling of a stream, continuous and melodious.

Of one thing I was sure. Whatever place that music came from was not only beautiful and peaceful, but also *happy*. There was no trace of sorrow in the music. It spoke of pure, rich, undying joy. It comforted, it inspired, it enthralled.

For an hour or so that music sang itself into my heart, lifting me above my sorrow, then it faded and I heard it no more. But I can never forget the wonder of it. Some day I hope to hear it again.

* * *

The empty nest

WHEREVER there are children in the family, life is rather noisy and the home is often in disorder. Toys, books, shoes and many other articles are scattered about, all of them a reproach to an orderly housewife, yet all of them precious signs of joyous, turbulent life. But one by one the children grow up and leave the home with quiet and tidy rooms.

How often as a young mother I despaired of ever keeping the house as I should like it. There was a time, while the children were small, when just crossing a room was almost like an obstacle race, for wooden building bricks lay in all directions and one had to pick one's way amongst them. After bricks came the era of toy trains and cars, with books piled up here and there to represent stations or garages. With the advent of a daughter, dolls and prams were added to the boys' toys, and when we seemed snowed under with toys, school-books appeared and silence descended for a few minutes at a time while the children laboriously wrote their first words in their copy-books.

With the children at school there would just be time to clean and tidy the house and get a meal ready, but a few minutes later the room would again be strewn with their latest interest. I well remember when the philatelist fever caught my second son. For some weeks we seemed to live in a sea of stamps, and day after day I found dozens of them lying soaking in the bath, waiting to be eased off the bit of paper to which they were stuck. I was even pressed into service to perform this duty myself!

The philatelist epoch was of short duration and gave way to painting. Designs and paintings lay around waiting to dry, and meanwhile I spent hours with a bottle of turpentine getting surplus colour off clothes and furniture. Then interest in painting faded suddenly and was replaced by music, not only playing music but composing it too. Sheets of music-paper with notes penned in lay all over the place and *must not be mixed up,* said my son.

Then, in turn, at 18 years of age, the children left home to prepare for their vocation as officers in The Salvation Army. And the home was quiet and oh, so tidy, for my husband and I long ago learned habits of order.

Many of my readers will already have passed through this experience of the gradual emptying of the nest of fledglings, and they will have adjusted themselves as we did to the quiet, serene happiness of a married couple who have weathered both joys and sorrows together for many years and whose lives have become pleasantly interwoven.

For some of us a precious child has left home under other and sadder circumstances. The angel of death has passed and taken a little one to be with God. The place is empty, so empty. . . . The house is still. No more toys litter the floor, no more school-books pile up on the table, no more quick footsteps bound up the stairs.

Is there any comfort for such a loss? Yes, there is. With all my heart I believe that what we call death is only transition, only the opening—and shutting—of a door, and that on the other side of that door is *life,* joyous, full, abounding life, rich in ways unimaginable to our finite minds. Your child, my child, is there, awaiting our coming.

* * *

Facing widowhood

DEATH is the one inevitable fact of human life. Having entered the scene we have to make an exit, yet how little that last fact colours our thoughts and plannings. The passing of a loved one always brings a trauma from which it takes time to recover. Happy are they whose hands are linked firmly with the heavenly Father's and who believe in the ongoingness of life beyond the portal we call death. How meaningless life would be if death were the end!

When my husband died, after 40 years of married partnership, I said immediately to myself: 'Now you have joined the vast number of widows. You are not alone in your bereavement. Thousands have passed this way before you and have triumphed over their sorrows and difficulties, many of them facing far worse circumstances than you do, having a young family to provide for.' My first resolution was: 'I will not complain. I will fight any tendency to self-pity with all my strength. I will remember *what I still have,* despite my sore loss.'

Many were praying for me and I thank them again now. It is difficult to assess how much strength and grace is released through intercessory prayer, but there is quite definitely a very real surge of power available through the upholding by friends of one in need.

From the moment when I fully accepted the fact that my dear one had died, a warmth of sustaining grace seemed to fill me. It was as though my husband companioned me, particularly when I walked in the garden or in the park opposite our home. There was a joyful recognition that he had passed through an unseen veil into the wider, more satisfying life of the spirit, yet I felt that he walked by my side, bringing a kind of exultation to my heart despite my aloneness.

This sense of his presence lasted for about 10 days and then it faded, but what comfort and serenity it brought me! Others have told me that they, too, have had this feeling of actual presence and quiet joy after the passing of loved ones. I am quite sure that it is a gift of God in His infinite goodness. The loss is there, the physical weariness after the strain, the mental burden of taking over all the ensuing problems, but one is encircled by the everlasting arms of divine love.

For days afterward, as I worked at home with all the details that follow bereavement, I hummed to myself the old song:

> *There is grace enough when the way is rough,*
> *There is grace enough when the fight is tough;*
> *'Tis a promise I claim in Jesus' name,*
> *There's grace enough . . . for me.*

Gradually one has to tackle the sorting out of clothes and other belongings. What poignant memories are awakened and what heart-stabs bring pain. It is not the newly-acquired articles that speak the loudest but the old ones: the well-worn slippers, the old cardigan, the much-used wallet.

One temptation that any bereaved person must resist is to live in the past in thought. Life must go on! Gratitude for the past is real and constant, but one must live in the present, picking up those threads of daily life that remain and weaving in new threads of additional duties and interests.

Every day I thank God for His goodness. How people can face life's blows without the solid rock of Christian belief beneath their feet I do not know. Our gracious God meets us in our hour of need.

* * *

Confessions of a grandma

NO remorse fills my heart as I write these confessions. No contrition wrinkles my brow (though age has done so) and no false modesty can withhold me from the statements I am about to make.

Firstly, very simply, I am grandma to the most wonderful baby in the whole world. And I am *proud* of that fact. But is not pride a besetting sin? If so, I am culpable. I shall have to use picture language to tell you how I felt on reaching this new and dignified status. Had I been a bird I should have winged far up in the highest heaven and poured out my exultant song. Had I been a rosebud I should have opened instantaneously into a perfect flower, filling the room with my fragrance. Had I been a balloon I should have swelled until I burst!

But I was none of these. I was just an ordinary woman to whom this great joy came. What did I do? I did like the woman in Christ's parable of the lost coin. I called on my neighbours to rejoice with me. Only I did it in the modern manner, over the phone. A granddaughter. Alive and kicking. Healthy and whole. Mother and child doing marvellously. What a thrill to be able to give the good news!

Of course, my friends already knew that a great event was in the offing. I could not keep the joyous news to myself. Overflowing with my delicious secret I confided first to one and then another that I should have to be extra careful of my health, for I was an expectant grandmother.

And so the long waiting time began. With both land and sea separating us, my daughter and I wove the old familiar pattern in the form of letters. What to eat or avoid. What to wear. What to prepare. And a hundred other small, intimate details.

What clothes does a new baby need? What are the minimum requirements in the way of equipment? What *does* a new baby wear nowadays? I remember the hand-knitted crossover vests that were the fashion when my first-born arrived. And the long robes he started in. But he was born in England many years ago. My other two children were born in Sweden and had quite a different outfit. They were packed up in parcels, if you understand what I mean. With feet enclosed in the outer covering and a steadying broad linen belt tied round the middle. It certainly made them easier to pick up, as it gave them the firm compactness that a new-born otherwise lacks.

When the first excitement of the news of the new arrival had cooled, another feeling gripped me. A quieter, almost awed mood. Thankfulness to God for a safe deliverance for the young mother and her child. And then wonder—wonder at the miracle of life. I was a link in the chain of the generations of the world. Having received life, I had passed it on, and now my child held her own new-born to her breast. Mystery of mysteries. Out of the great unknown we come, one by one. Back into the beyond we are gathered when our lifespan is at an end.

Of course, I haven't seen the little marvel yet, but I heard her voice over the phone when she was only a week old. Honesty compels me to state that it was a trifle insistent and loud. I hope she will learn to modify it when she grows older. Naturally, I have received photographs of her. It is a cause for real thanksgiving on my part that she does not resemble me in the least. Believe it or not, she is a darling.

Learning early that it is better to give than to receive, she cooed and chuckled in a tape for me for Christmas. No one else around here understands her language of sounds, but I do. She is saying: 'Here I am, dear Grandma, safely arrived in this jolly old world. What a lark to be alive, to suck your toes and splash in the bath.'

And much more. Some of it in a minor key, stridently revealing a funny, empty feeling inside and . . . isn't it time we had supper?

My final confession is that I am secretly practising being a grandma. I borrow other people's babies to feel their weight and size up their condition and age. Folk in the supermarket see a grey-haired woman trundling her purchases in a trolley. They have no imagination! I'm wheeling little Anne. Dextrously getting the pram round the corners of heaped-up tins of food and steering in the direction of the fruit. One needs some practice after 20 years without pram-pushing.

One thing makes me a little anxious. The world does not always appear to be the best place for small children to grow up. Scanning the headlines of the morning news makes one apprehensive. So much wrong-doing. So much unmerited suffering. So much heart-break. And bright-eyed, rosy-cheeked babies have to grow up to face life's burdens. Will mankind never learn the lesson that it must love or perish? My prayers enfold my grandchild daily. May she be one of God's answers to the world's problems.

Hunger

HUNGER!
What is hunger?
It is craving after bread
It is aching after food,
An empty, painful sucking in the vitals;
A deadly hate 'gainst those who have
And do not share . . .
Hunger!

Hunger!
What is hunger?
It is craving after love
It is longing for a kiss,
A painful yearning for a dear one's arms,
A wee child's loving hug,
A baby's smile . . .
Heart hunger!

Hunger!
What is hunger?
It is searching after light
It is longing to be good,
A deep heart-hunger after righteousness,
To know the Father's will . . .
For more of God.
Soul hunger!

15

Life's basic needs

WHAT are the basic needs to support human life? We get the answer when we consider what a criminal used to be given as punishment—a diet of bread and water. It was enough to sustain life but no more. The bread and water was only a meagre response to man's most primitive cravings—hunger and thirst.

Jesus referred to these fundamental needs when He declared: 'I am the bread of life: he that cometh to me shall never hunger; and he that believeth on me shall never thirst' (John 6:35).

Hunger . . . thirst . . . not physical here but spiritual. Soul hunger and thirst, what is that? It is the yearning for goodness, for holiness, for rectitude of life and conduct, which is found in the man or woman conscious of a longing after God. This desire for righteousness can become a predominant hunger, taking first place over other legitimate cravings of the human spirit for love, friendship, understanding and self-expression.

We live in a mechanized age when everything works to time-tables, even our meals. Doctors assure us that regularity is a good thing, but have you ever thought of our forefathers who had to hunt animals or catch birds or fish before they could eat?

Think of the cave-man setting off with his club, leaving his wife and children with empty stomachs waiting for his return. In those days they knew what hunger meant. Nowadays, when we catch a nice smell of cooking coming from the kitchen we say: 'Oh, I'm hungry . . .', but I don't suppose any of us know what real hunger is.

Hunger, though a primary appetite of the body, is not always present. During an illness the appetite disappears. That is a danger sign that the body is not working normally. In the same way, if we feel no special hunger our soul-life is in danger.

Too little activity lessens the appetite. We who have brought up children know the improvement in their appetites when they come in from playing in the fresh air. It just seems they will never stop eating. Yet a few days indoors for some reason or another lessens the need for food and the children have to be coaxed to eat. To have spiritual hunger we must have some spiritual activity; we must be serving God in some way. Even the house-bound can pray for others and thus help them.

How does hunger after God manifest itself? By what signs can we know it? It is a sense of emptiness, a lack of meaning in life, however busy we are. Some people do not recognize the gnawing ache of the heart as God-hunger. They try to fill their hours with extra work, pleasures, friendships, ambitions, but all is of no use while the soul is unsatisfied.

When I was young I knew a deep longing for the fullness of God, and I imagined that if I sought with sufficient zeal and intensity God would grant me an experience which would satisfy me for ever afterwards, so that never again should I feel any spiritual lack. In maturity I believe that this hunger and thirst of the soul must be a daily appetite for more of God. We can never stock up a spiritual store cupboard full of supplies then cease to pray or seek God daily, feeling that we have plenty in our reserves to carry us through for a few weeks.

It is so with daily food. Sometimes, as a busy housewife, I should have liked to say to my husband and children: 'Eat plenty today, for there won't be any more food for three days, while I do the spring-cleaning.' But I knew that could never be carried through. A daily intake for a daily outgo is the rule of life.

There is much talk of counting calories so as not to put on weight or cause illness. That danger does not exist with spiritual sustenance. We can never have too much of God; too much of His love, power or mercy. The danger is always the opposite—that we try to get by on too little and our souls are undernourished and even starved.

Jesus also used the metaphor of thirst to denote the longing for God. We miss a lot of the deeper meaning of many Bible texts because we have so little personal knowledge of a hot and dry land, where water or its lack means the difference between life and death. Once in Argentina we travelled through a desert by bus. We were advised not to speak during the journey, to keep our mouths shut, with, if possible, a scarf over it. The windows of the bus were tightly closed yet a coating of fine sand soon covered us. Outside we saw a forest of giant cacti, themselves heavy with sand, while white birds flitted between them, pecking at the shoots and buds. As we journeyed in silence our mouths and throats dried out and it was a great relief to arrive at journey's end and be able to drink and drink . . . washing off the sand from our faces and necks and brushing it off our clothes. After a couple of hours in a desert landscape we can perhaps better appreciate the intensity of the psalmist's cry: 'My soul thirsteth after God, after the living God.'

Hunger . . . thirst . . . life's basic requirements for the soul can be met if we come to the One who can satisfy our needs. But we must come with faith, with earnest desire, with longing.

When in Santiago, Chile, I went one day with the social services truck to distribute hot soup to crowds of very poor children on the outskirts of the city. As the truck neared the area its horn gave several long blasts and immediately dozens of children started to run towards us. It was winter and the wind was cold, yet many of the children were barefoot and in rags. They poured out from their so-called homes in the shanty town, homes which were just a few planks of wood put roughly together or sheets of old corrugated iron, the holes stuffed with newspapers.

The children all carried some kind of a container. Some struggled with big saucepans, some came with small ones. One tiny girl in rags carried a large mug. A boy came with a frying pan. A long queue was formed and we helpers stood at the back of the truck ladling good hot soup into the receptacles held out to us. Each child received as much soup as would go in his or her pot. Some got a lot, some a little. It was unjust, you think? But it was inevitable. We who ladled out the soup could not give more than the pot could hold, and even then a small safety margin had to be left for carrying. I can still see the careful steps of the boy who balanced a frying pan filled with soup.

The little girl of about five with the mug duly got her share, but I wished it could have been more. She looked so cold and hungry. As I took one saucepan to fill I noticed a lump of something in the

63

bottom, and presuming it was an old potato I pulled it out, only to realize with consternation that it was a ball of old rags stuffed into a hole in the bottom. How many stews had been cooked on those old rags? I hastily pressed the unsavoury wet clump back into place and covered it with soup.

As we come to the Lord each day with our needs and longings, conscious of our insufficiencies, we must realize that God can't give us more than we have room for. If our faith is weak, if our sense of need is small, if our desire is feeble, then we shall receive but little. If our hearts are filled with self-interests then there will not be room for the infilling which otherwise the Lord might give us.

I think back to Chile again—to the soup distribution to poor children—and see before my mind's eye the waiting, expectant faces before the steaming cauldron. As the Lord looks down upon us at this moment, how does He see us? Are we looking up to Him in expectancy, in strong desire—hunger and thirst? If so, then our faith will be rewarded and He will grant us that which we need.

16

The Mercy Seat

NO Salvation Army hall is complete without a Mercy Seat. The first orders and regulations published in 1886 stated: 'Forms without backs may be kept close to the platform, simply pulled out, and the Mercy Seat is ready.' We have travelled a long way since that day. Look at our modern Mercy Seats, some of them resplendent with polished wood, protective cords slotted through posts and a beautiful carpet, with a small table in the centre bearing a bouquet of choice flowers.

I wonder if that mat knows that it is 'a chosen mat, a kingly mat, a holy mat, a peculiar mat'? I wonder if it suffers from a superiority complex, saying: 'I thank my God that I am not as other mats, dirty, torn, tramped on by feet of men. I am cleaned twice in the week. No rough shoes tread my royal surface for I am reverently kneeled upon . . . a most holy mat, set apart'? How does that mat feel when penitents kneel upon it? Does it resent any intrusion of its privacy and separateness, especially if the seeker is not too well clad? Or is it glad, glad with a deep humble gladness?

And does the flower-display table feel superior? In my childhood I saw the holiness table in use. It was just a small wooden table, which served at other times to mark the star-cards in the Sunday school, but one Sunday morning it held an honoured place in front of the platform, covered by a crimson cloth. On such occasions it was always referred to as the holiness table, and in my childish fancy it became a thing apart. When I saw uniformed Salvationists kneeling there, I wondered how they dared to approach such holy ground.

Our Mercy Seat is not a confessional. It is not a place to which we have to come again and again at set intervals. We can be both saved and sanctified without ever having knelt there, but for most of us it is the place we have sought in our spiritual crises. Blest Mercy Seat!

God speaks in many ways

IN the stillness of the rosy dawn,
In the hush that broods o'er vale and sea,
Comes the whisper of the Saviour's tender voice:
    Peace like this my love can bring thee.

In the ripple of the sunlit brook,
In the glorious sight of flow'ring tree,
In the laughter of a child I hear my Lord:
    Joy like this I long to give thee.

In the cleaving of the frozen soil
When the call of spring is heard with glee,
In the bursting of the bud, God speaks His word:
    Life abundant I will grant thee.

In the quiet trust of ageing saints
Who have borne life's blows so patiently,
Comes God's promise to my faint and falt'ring heart:
    Grace sufficient I'll accord thee.

17

Hold your tongue!

THE first time I became aware of the link between tongue and talk was in my first class at school. Some of the children had been chattering and the teacher hit upon an original way of punishing offenders. On several sheets of brown paper she drew a long red tongue, sticking them together until the tongue measured about a yard in length. Then fixing the class with a stern eye she said: 'The very next child who speaks without permission will come out here in front of the class and stand with this tongue pinned to her clothes.'

Sure enough, after a few moments the awful warning had been forgotten by one child. Forward to the front she must go, and during the remainder of the class she stood there bearing the shameful badge of the long red tongue.

What talkers some people are! Schooldays over we find even more to say. It has been reckoned that on average we talk about five hours a day. So many words would make a book of 500 pages in a week. A big, heavy book, full of . . . what? Very little of importance.

In the third chapter of the Epistle of James he writes of the tongue as something that no man can tame, and goes on to say: 'Therewith bless we God . . . and therewith curse we men' (v9). What a responsibility is speech! The sins of silence are very few compared with the sins of speech.

We are so used to the mass media spreading news to us from all quarters of the globe that we can hardly credit how fast gossip travels on the tongues of people. It has been calculated that if someone hearing a piece of scandal told two other persons about it within 15 minutes, and these two passed it on, each to two others, and so on, the whole world would know it by next day.

Words! O the power of them! Words that heal and help, bless and comfort; that fall as balm on a wounded spirit and dry the tears from sorrowful eyes. Would that we all spoke more words like that!

But there is another use for the tongue; an abased use—the spewing out of abrasive words intended to cut, to hurt, to tear apart; words that are like knives, sharpened on the strop of an unforgiving spirit. May God forgive us for such words if we have spoken them.

For *words have power!* They do not fall on empty air, to be carried away by a passing breeze. They have a life of their own. They pierce deep into sensitive souls, into depressed spirits, into impressionable minds. They can provide the right growing ground or they can hinder, devitalize and cripple. A whole lifetime ahead someone may remember a remark we made quite casually today; remember it with gratitude for the boost it gave, or blame us for dampening out a spark of initiative, a good resolve, or jeering at the thought of some act of kindly service.

There is playful talk. Happy, kindly banter, little quips and jokes, family fun that cheers the day along on smooth wheels. Among friends or workmates such words brighten the eyes and lighten up the face, acting like a tonic.

What a joy for parents to teach a child its first words. With what patience the sounds are encouraged over and over again until the baby lips can form the complete word. The thrill of it! Today baby said: 'Mam-ma, Dad-da.' What excited listener to the little marvel could possibly visualize the same child two years later, talking all day long from morn to night with endless chatter and questions, until the exasperated parent, wearied beyond endurance, snarls: 'Now you've learnt to talk, shut up!'

Jesus Himself warned about the misuse of the tongue. 'But I say unto you, That every idle word that men shall speak, they shall give account thereof in the day of judgment. For by thy words thou shalt be justified, and by thy words thou shalt be condemned' (Matthew 12:36, 37).

When I was a teenager it was the fashion to recite poems in public, and some lines from one of the favourites come back to me:

> *Boys flying kites haul in their white-winged birds,*
> *But you can't do that when you're flying words.*

68

Have you heard of the Trappist monks who take a vow of silence, so as not to sin in speech? It is said that the only allowed greeting is: 'Brother, you must die.' That is a hard rule and should not be applied to daily life for those of us in the great pulsating world of everyday. We need to meet and greet our fellowmen, using our speech wisely and thoughtfully, lightly and cheerily, briefly and happily, as we pass on our way.

What issues from our lips will depend on what lies in our hearts and minds. Jesus reminded His hearers that 'a man's words will always express what has been treasured in his heart' (Luke 6:45, Phillips). What are we most interested in?—our new hobby, our work, family ties, gardening or embroidery . . . it doesn't matter what it is. If we are full of it, it will slip into our speech and colour our talk, until perhaps our friends are bored stiff with it! And when Christ fills the heart some word of witness, some expression of confidence in Him, of trust in His loving care, will have its place in our conversation, unforced and without embarrassment.

Some people are tongue-tied! They wish they could talk fluently and easily on any subject, but words fail them and they listen enviously to those who have 'the gift of the gab'. If we are listeners rather than talkers, don't despair. We will escape many temptations and it is probable that what we do say is of greater value, being quality rather than quantity.

The story-teller, Hans Andersen, of Denmark, wrote of a house-troll who was tongue-tied. The quaint little gnome who lived un-seen in a home and took lively interest in all the family's doings and sayings would have loved to spin yarns to his troll-friends about his housefolk, but every time he tried to describe them he stuttered and hesitated, then fell silent, blushing with shame. But the house-mother, she could talk! From morning to night she rattled on about every conceivable subject, and her flow of words was majestic and turbulent and rippling . . . a very crescendo of sound.

One night, when the family had gone to bed, the little troll decided to borrow the housewife's tongue from her mouth and use it himself, just for the night hours, of course, while she was asleep. And what a lovely time he had. The tongue was so long and so red, so full of words, that its new owner—or rather borrower—could astonish his friends with the most magnificent flights of rhetoric. By morning the troll tucked the long red tongue back into its owner's mouth, giving it a small tug to make sure it was properly fastened. And strangely enough next day the poor woman found herself not tongue-tied but tongue-*tired*, and had little to say for herself. This became the pattern for her life, though she never found out why!

No, do not be anxious! Let us sleep in peace, for no one will ever borrow our tongue. Each of us is responsible for its use or misuse. Perhaps it would be a good idea if each morning we all prayed this prayer: 'Set a watch, O Lord, before my mouth; keep the door of my lips' (Psalm 141:3).

18

Lost car keys

ONE Sunday afternoon in France, as my husband and I were driving home from some meetings, our route took us near to the famous Chartres Cathedral, renowned for its spectacular stained-glass windows. We decided to visit it. After being shown round the inside, my husband—an ardent photographer—took pictures of the stately edifice from different viewpoints. When we returned to the car my husband broke the ominous news that the keys were missing from his pocket. Immediately, we separated to search the whole area.

Hundreds of other tourists were milling around but we searched, as well as we could, each spot we had visited. After half an hour we met again, only to report failure. We decided to try a little longer before going home by train to get the spare keys, which of course I ought to have had with me.

Standing on the pavement I prayed desperately: 'Lord, You know where those keys are. Help me to find them.' The thought came to me to enquire whether there was a lost property office nearby, and looking for someone to ask I felt a strong impulse to approach a policeman on traffic duty at busy crossroads. I had to wait some time while he whistled the cars forward, then in a lull I crossed to his island in mid-street and put my question.

'What have you lost?' he enquired. I confessed it was the car keys.

'What make is your car and how many keys were there?' was his next question, which I answered rapidly, as more cars were queueing up behind him.

To my utter surprise he fished in his trouser pocket and brought out the missing keys, handing them to me with a smile. He had found them on the pavement as he came on duty earlier.

Shortages

LORD, gloom is in the air,
    prophets of doom abound.
The world is running short of
    vital products;
Its natural resources are being depleted
    at a rapid rate.
We are living above our means,
Drawing heavily on the few pounds we still have
    in the energy bank.

At such a time, Master, it is good
    to remind ourselves
That Your spiritual resources are limitless.
Your bounties are immeasurable,
    Your love all-embracing.
It gives such inward security to know
    that if all else fails,
      You do not fail.
If all else goes, *You remain.*

Thank You, Lord, for that certainty
Which can keep my heart at peace,
    cradled in Your care.

19

God's resources

HAVE any of us ever felt depressed? Really down in spirit as though all the world was against us . . . as though we would never again become happy or fulfilled? I am sure we all have. None of us escapes those awful moments when the stuffing seems to sag out of us, the air goes out of our energy balloon, and the joy and faith of our Christian beliefs is overclouded by dense billows of uncertainty and even doubt. It is at such moments that we need to remind ourselves of God's unlimited resources of power, of renewal.

A friend of mine told me that when serving God abroad she had reached such a point of depression that she could hardly continue with her duties. Looming on the dark horizon, however, was a God-given shaft of light—an invitation to attend a missionary conference in that area.

In the first gathering the leader quoted Paul's words to the Philippians: 'But my God shall supply all your need according to his riches in glory by Christ Jesus' (Philippians 4:19). He then went on to say that each person attending the conference had some special spiritual need, some lack in their life or service of which they were painfully conscious. They were asked to think in silence for a moment to decide which was their greatest need. Was it for more patience, more love, more faith? Or better relationships with co-workers? After the silence the leader passed round pieces of paper and asked each one to write down his or her greatest need.

Then they took up the collection! Not an ordinary money collection. As the plate was passed round, each one gave the folded paper on which he or she had written. The leader raised the plate in his two hands and prayed: 'O God! You see our great needs. Supply them now according to Your riches in glory by Christ Jesus. Amen.'

My friend said that as he prayed those words a sense of relief, of joy, of renewed faith, swept through her heart. Some blockage had been pierced, had been removed. The simple ceremony of pinpointing the chief lack, writing it down and having it presented to God publicly, became the key which opened her struggling soul once again to God's light and power.

If we had been present that day, what would we have written on the paper? This is such a personal matter that perhaps we could not open our heart to another. We all feel a sense of need and shortcoming in our spiritual experience. But God is rich, abundantly rich, and moreover willing to give us that which we require. Our problem is to learn how to receive from God.

There is a vast spiritual universe outside this physical and material world of ours. It encircles us, impinges upon our lives, influencing us and aiding us in the measure in which we are open and receptive to it. To believe in God theoretically is one thing. To believe so deeply that all one's life is affected thereby is quite another. We are faced with a human disability. We cannot make easy contact with divine power. Surely the basis of the charismatic revival lay in the fact that people had begun to learn *how to receive from God.* How to open themselves to the power of the Spirit, to the inflowing of divine resources.

When I was a child the first crystal radio sets were creating great interest. Most of them were made at home. My elder brother assembled the necessary parts which included earphones, as in those days there were no loudspeakers. He bought the fine needle and the small glittering crystal. One day is imprinted on my memory. My brother stood with the earphones on, moving the 'cat's whisker' from point to point of the crystal, trying to find a sensitive spot. We others round him were anxiously watching his face and asking: 'Can you hear anything?' A negative shake of the head was his reply. Suddenly his face lit up. 'I've got it!' he said. I clamoured for my turn at listening and the earphones were adjusted. Then for the first time in my life I heard music from the air. I trembled with excitement. The thrill of that moment still grips me! Music in the very air of our old-fashioned dining-room with its dark furniture and heavy curtains. It had been there all the time and we hadn't known it. Music . . . and words . . . and more music. Fantastic! A harvest from the ether at will, if only one could make connection. That experience is now commonplace and today's children think nothing of it.

Some years later, when I married, we had a battery radio. We lived in London and every Friday evening a lad used to call with a newly-filled accumulator, which I remember as an evil-looking glass box filled with dark liquid and plates. We handed over the flat accumulator and paid twopence for the refilled one, which lasted us about a week. Towards the end of that time, as the battery started to run down, the sound got fainter and we had to bend over it to catch what was said. At times we had to turn off the radio and miss some programmes, so as to be able to listen to others. A kind of self-rationing system.

Some people's spiritual batteries are filled up once a week, mostly on Sundays in church or meeting hall, and they expect to be able to live on that supply for a week. They have not learnt how to receive *daily* from God for their soul's needs.

How can we learn to receive from God and to open our lives more fully to Him? How can we link our weakness to His inexhaustible strength and imbibe in fuller measure His love, His joy, His serenity and power? What can we do to increase our receptivity from God? Is our spiritual attunement faulty? Is our soul's aerial disconnected? Can we not plug in permanently to an unfailing supply from an infinite source? Is there some know-how that we have not learnt? How eager is our search?

My own answers—partial though they be—lie along three lines. First, I have found God focused in Christ in the Gospels, that divine and central Figure striding through the records. Jesus Christ, mysterious and challenging; Carpenter, Prophet, Teacher and Healer, Preacher of the Kingdom of Heaven. To learn more of Him, to sense His controlled power, to follow Him through the dusty human scenes, is to be stirred to one's depths. He had the secret of immediate vital communion with God His Father. Can we not learn it from Him?

Then I have found God increasingly in nature. In many people's thinking God is still resting after the seventh day of creation, but Jesus revealed Him to be in continuous activity. 'My Father has never yet ceased his work, and I am working too' (John 5:17, *NEB*). This surge of life around us, in all forms of being, affects us continually. We must strive to attune to its ceaseless rhythm. God, Primal Source of life, holds the threads of all being in His hands. We are part of His creation and cannot dissociate ourselves from its other forms. Through a flower, a tree, a stretch of sky, the path of the wind, God has spoken to me.

Finally, I have found God becoming more real in prayer. In the silence of worship or meditation we open avenues into our soul along which God can approach. And coming, He brings strength and joy into our own lives, and guidance and power for our service for Him.

I remember one Easter Sunday morning when in my quiet devotional time I had praised the Lord of Life, the Resurrected Christ, my Lord and Master. As I sat with eyes closed but face uplifted, yielding myself as far as I knew how to the presence and incoming of God's Spirit, a surge of joy thrilled through all my being. For some brief moments I felt myself seized, invaded, by the Spirit of God, filled with joy and love and a sense of mental, physical and spiritual well-being. Would that such spiritual quickenings came more often!

In Central Chile, where we lived for three years, the summer is one long six-month period of sunshine and blue skies after the comparative cold of winter. During those months not a single drop of rain falls, so there is no problem with arranging outings, picnics or holidays. But such brilliant weather exacts a certain toll. The grass on the hills dries to brown straw. Dust on the hedgerows becomes so thick that individual leaves cannot be discerned. If you want a few flowers in your garden you must water three times a day.

Despite the long drought Central Chile is renowned for its wonderful vegetables, fruit and flowers. How can these flourish without rain? The secret lies high in the Andes Mountains covered by eternal snow in a thick white blanket. The heat of the sun melts sufficient of the snow to send fresh, cold, life-giving streams down to the valleys, where irrigation canals convey it to the orchards and fields. Soon the precious liquid is running through thousands of smaller channels to individual farms.

We watched the farmer as he rode on horseback around his acres, opening a narrow stream here, shutting one there by the simple means of throwing in some stones and earth, and thus getting the best distribution of the water at his disposal. If any field was left dry it was the farmer's fault, who had not attended properly to the irrigation. The water was there to be had but the canal was blocked.

This is a telling illustration of God's eternal resources at our disposal if we will but receive them. Like the farmer we can easily put blockages into the way of accepting what God offers us. It may just be carelessness, not giving God a chance to meet our needs; it may be lack of prayer or faith, or self-centredness.

Let us come back to the text we started with: 'My God shall supply all your need according to his riches in glory by Christ Jesus.' Did each of us mentally note down something as our greatest need? Just there God can meet us if we will open our lives fully to Him.

Awkward saints

I CAN love sinners, for my heart is stirred to feel
    they have no one
to whom to turn in those deep sorrows
and perplexities which shade our lives.

All are not conscious of their lack of God.
    Some with merry hearts
fritter away the gifts entrusted to them;
    some mock, some doubt, some laugh;
but my heart yearns to introduce them
    to the Best of Friends.

I *do* love sinners, yet 'tis strange, O Lord,
how difficult I find the *awkward* saints!
    The love I feel for those
outside Your fold seems somehow lacking
when it is Your own who irritate me.
We expect so much of those who name Your Name,
that we forget the human vessel's frailty
    and our sight is jaundiced
by our ready misconception of motives
    seen alone by You
and judged at their true worth.

Dear Lord, increase my love,
until its blaze shall burn unkindly criticism
    from my soul;
until its power shall soothe all pricks
resulting from my walk with fellow-men.

20

What shall I wear?

ONE of a woman's greatest daily questions is: What shall I wear? Probably the first worry of each morning is what to put on for that day. In 'Woman's Hour' on the radio one afternoon I heard a young girl who had recently joined a military unit say: 'It's simply marvellous not to have to think all the time of what to wear, knowing it will be the same old uniform.' It has been heard of a woman, surveying her crammed wardrobe, to declaim tragically: 'I've nothing to wear!'

On Independence Day in Finland it is the custom for the president to hold a gala reception at the palace in Helsinki to which government ministers, ambassadors and wives, religious and military leaders and other special guests are invited. The Salvation Army leader and his wife are included in the chosen number, so for seven years my husband and I represented Finnish Salvationists for that great event at the palace. Each of the hundreds of guests was received personally by the president with a handshake and a smile, sometimes a few words of greeting. One woman—a designer of fashionable clothes—regularly made a stage entry, delaying just a few seconds before sweeping a deep curtsey. Her choice of evening dress was always one of the points most discussed. I remember watching her trip forward one year looking like a setting sun in a glorious blaze of red, which must have taken some courage to wear, even for a noted dress designer.

The biggest sensations were caused by the various foreign ambassadors and their wives, and the pageant of colour and style, the flash of diamonds, the sheen of pearls, the awe-inspiring array of medals, made it a noble sight. Our Army uniforms looked very plain and business-like in that sparkling crowd, but how happy I was that I did not have to worry about what to wear. During the gala one year a rather comical incident occurred in the crowded halls of the palace. One young woman wore a backless evening

gown, adorned with a huge ribbon rosette—at least a foot across—
at the back waist. A much-decorated military officer, trying to pass
her in the crush, caught some of his medals in her rosette and nearly
tore it off. Bystanders had to come to the rescue and free the two
unhappily-linked guests.

What shall I wear? Each woman must answer her own question
as far as daily dress is concerned, but Paul offers us some advice as
to the spiritual garments we should seek to own. He begins with a
choice phrase: 'Put on the garments that suit God's chosen people,
his own, his beloved: compassion, kindness, humility, gentleness,
patience. Be forbearing . . . and forgiving. . . . To crown all, there
must be love, to bind all together' (Colossians 3:12-14, *NEB*).

What beautiful clothes these are! What lovely soft raiment! I
imagine them in pastel colours and quite naturally crease-resistant.
Wear these spiritual garments and how much easier the daily home
or work relationships will be. Some people are hard, self-centred,
with awkward angles sticking out all over them, tearing others to
shreds. There is so much selfishness, bitterness and resentment
between people that we need the love of Christ in our hearts, we
need to wear 'the garments that suit God's chosen people', to
counter-balance and perhaps overcome the evil around us.

Robert Louis Stevenson tells the story of two maiden sisters in
the Edinburgh of long ago:

> 'This pair', he said, 'inhabited a single room. From the facts it must have been
> double-bedded and it may have been of some dimensions. But it was a single
> room. Here our two spinsters fell out, fell out so bitterly that there was never a
> word spoken between them from that day forward. You would have thought that
> they would separate, but no, whether from lack of means or the Scottish fear of
> scandal, they continued to keep house together. A chalk line on the floor
> separated their domains. It bisected the doorway and the stove so that they could
> go in and out and do their cooking, without violating the territory of the other.
> So for years they co-existed in a state of hateful silence. At night in the dark
> watches, each could hear the other breathe. But not one word did they exchange
> with each other, and at length the hand of death put an even stronger barrier of
> silence between them.'

What a tragedy! To go into eternity with an unforgiving spirit
searing the soul. Yet it is not always easy to 'be forbearing and
forgiving'. Pride rears its ugly head and says: 'It was her fault, not
yours. Don't you take the first step to make amends. Let her come
and apologize. You stand firm!' That is the devil's advice and it is
fatal to good relationships. Paul counsels us: 'Do not let anger lead

you into sin; do not let sunset find you still nursing it' (Ephesians 4:26, *NEB*). To nurse anger is to nurse a venomous snake in our heart. We may hope it will strike the one we consider an enemy, but make no mistake, its fangs will also fasten into us and poison us.

With that ugly picture of an unforgiving spirit in our minds, with what relief we turn to the spiritual garments suggested by Paul: 'compassion, kindness, humility, gentleness, patience . . .' [with] 'love, to bind all together'.

We can learn to forgive others only when we ourselves have been forgiven by Christ, when His love has broken down the hard core of anger within and melted our bitter spirit. I had an unforgettable illustration of that during my years in France.

In connection with an evangelistic campaign in Nice, on the Mediterranean, I was the guest of a woman who lived alone. It was a beautiful, typically French home, with large rooms filled with old-fashioned, well-polished furniture. My hostess was middle-aged and exceedingly kind, but I noticed immediately with a shiver of horror that her face was drawn down on one side by some terrible scars. Perhaps the result of a traffic accident, I thought.

While we drank a cup of tisane, the herb tea used so much in France, she spoke to me of her joy in the recently-opened Salvation Army corps in Nice, where she had been enrolled as a soldier. Her face shone with God's peace in spite of the disfigurement. Suddenly she said: 'You see how scarred I am. Have you time to hear what happened?' I assured her that I had and her strange story began.

'I was a happy wife and mother', she said, 'in this very house. That is my daughter . . .', and she handed me a photo of a teenage girl sitting playing a harp. 'One big cloud hung over our home life. My husband began to drink, sometimes coming home quite drunk. My daughter became ill and I nursed her at home, which took a lot of my time. I noticed that my husband seemed to become jealous of the hours I had to spend with the girl and he drank more and more.

'Then our daughter died and I was plunged into deep grief. The day after the funeral I sat at home crying when my husband burst in, drunken and angry. Seeing my tears he shouted: "You're still thinking about the girl and not about me", then he drew a revolver and shot at me several times. I woke up in hospital with bandages all over my face and in great pain. When the doctor came to my bedside I murmured: "What about my husband?" "He is dead", came the reply. "He put the last shot through his own head."'

'How I wished I had died too! But skilful nursing restored me and the day came when the bandages were taken off and I saw the terrible scars. From that moment I hated my husband with a deadly hatred. I came home and lived here, hardly ever going out except for some evening shopping, because of my scars. One night I saw a half-dozen people in strange dark uniforms standing on the pavement singing songs and inviting passers-by into a nearby hall for a meeting. I went in and found it was a newly-opened corps of The Salvation Army, of which I knew nothing. I enjoyed the singing and the Bible address and I longed for the peace and joy they spoke of.

'I continued to attend the small meetings and one evening I knelt at the small table at the front which they called the Mercy Seat and prayed for God's forgiveness for my sins. What happened was like a miracle! As I prayed and my tears flowed, the stone of hate and bitterness in my heart disappeared, and joy and peace enveloped me.'

The little woman finished her story. Both her eyes and mine were moist with tears but her face shone with what looked like divine glory. 'Now you understand why I am happy, despite my scars,' she added. 'God has forgiven me and I have forgiven my husband.'

That night, as I lay down to sleep, I felt I had been near the very portals of paradise, for I had seen the glory of the Lord in a scarred but radiant face.

What a wonderful garment is forgiveness! God's forgiveness of us and our forgiveness of others. May we wear it humbly and gratefully.

21

Quicksands

ALTHOUGH only a child I had heard of the fearful quicksands which could suck one down to a slow death by drowning. But that I should ever have experience of them I could not imagine.

As a reward for good behaviour, my father had taken me with him on a visit to the seaside. While he attended to business, I went with my new friend, the son of the house, down to the shore to play. We had a lovely time racing over the sand and jumping from rock to rock, becoming more and more reckless in our excitement.

Suddenly, as I jumped from one rock into the sand I felt it sink beneath my feet and water oozed around me. I tried to extricate myself but found I could not. Quicksands! In terror I called to the boy, 'Help! I'm sinking. . . .' He came running towards me, careful to jump from rock to rock. From the nearest one he stretched out his hand to me and drew me up beside him.

To this day I remember the sense of relief, of freedom, of safety, as I stood beside him on the rock, both of us panting with our exertions. Those moments for me were unforgettable.

Years later I found a description very similar in the first verses of the 40th Psalm, where David uses these words to describe his soul's experience:

'The Lord . . . inclined unto me, and heard me cry. He brought me up . . . out of the miry clay, and set my feet upon a rock. . . . He hath put a new song in my mouth, even praise unto our God.' How wonderful to know that when our feet tread sin's strangling quicksands, a cry for help to our Saviour can bring Him to our side and grant us deliverance.

Too small a saint

LORD, 'tis with shame I make my way to Thee;
With heavy heart I seek the holy place,
Ashamed to raise my eyes, afraid to look
    Into Thy face.

I'm not too great a sinner but I'm just
Too small a saint. Too easily I yield
And wound my soul by lightly speaking words
    Love had concealed.

So small a thing it needs to bring a cloud,
A look, a frown or an intolerant thought.
And there upon the whiteness of my soul
    A stain is wrought.

My soul has vision and would rise, be freed
Of all earth's selfish janglings; yet my wings
At times do fail me, and I sink, a prey
    To paltry things.

Have mercy on me, Lord, and in Thy grace
Pardon my pettiness, my feeble hold
On truths divine. Forgive my cowardice,
    Make me more bold.

More bold to fight the tempting thoughts that come
Unasked; more kind to folk who grate on me.
By constant watching may I daily grow
    To be like Thee.

22

The growing pains of sainthood

Saints abounding

IN The Salvation Army we have our saints. Big saints and little saints, placid saints and fiery saints, home saints and office saints, tongue-tied saints and preacher saints, men saints and women saints, born saints and born-again saints. What a mighty host! They speak different languages, their skin is of varied hue, their background multifarious, but one thing they have in common. In their lives Christ is first and Christ is last, and through their eyes shines God's love.

Their names have never appeared on any roll of saints; no marble effigies of them adorn our halls; they are not invoked to bless our campaigns, further our financial efforts or to intercede with God on our behalf. Their message has always been: 'Look not at me. I am but a voice, a messenger, for One greater than I. What He has done for me, He can do for you.'

What are the hallmarks of a true saint? And here I take the word 'saint' not in its New Testament implication of 'believer', but in its modern sense of 'a person eminent for piety and virtue' (Nuttall). Cruden gives this interesting definition: 'A holy or godly person by profession, covenant and conversation.' Do these terms create a picture of superhuman and isolated perfection, far removed from ordinary sinful, though seeking, mortals?

Is sainthood reserved for the élite? Is it a spiritual trademark guaranteeing the worth of chosen vessels? Is it only for those with inborn leanings toward pietism and with a character already stabilized before it became God-gripped?

The saints of all time have been flesh and blood like you and me. They have fought hard against external odds and even more desperately against the baser leanings of their own desires. Above all, they have learnt the secret of surrender, of full surrender to the Spirit of God. And the upsurge of God's Spirit in their hearts has purified and transformed their nature. From that moment they walk with God, humbly and obediently, until the divine is unmistakably stamped on their brow. Year by year they mature in grace and goodness and the fragrance of their lives spills over. 'Saints, like all masterpieces, are made slowly,' says René Bazin.

What are these saints like? Are they austere, unapproachable, in their holiness of life? Why no! Real saints are jolly people with twinkling eyes and a hearty hand-clasp. Their temperament may colour them as extrovert or introvert, but by one sign we know them: the mainspring of their lives is *love*; love to God and love to man.

Another distinguishing characteristic is that no true saint is aware of his sanctity. If you mention it to him he will protest vigorously, for it remains an axiom that the moment a person knows himself to be good, he ceases to be good. The saint himself is unconscious of the holy influence he wields and, all unknown to him, his features shine with a reflected glory that betrays the divine Indweller of his heart.

A third trait of the real saint is that he has arrived safely in the harbour of implicit faith in God. His frail barque has been blown by the winds of doubt against the rocks of doctrinal problems; he has known the eddies of personal disappointments and the perilous rapids of seemingly cruel blows of fate, but he has held his course.

Ponder what Albert Orsborn said: 'A saint is not a man without faults, but one who is big enough to confess them and go right on loving God in sincerity and truth.' That brings it down to a more earthly level, doesn't it? It gives us hope—for ourselves.

Making a saint is no easy job even for Almighty God. It takes time and effort on His part and ours, for we must co-operate. No man or woman becomes a saint while asleep.

I have been writing about *real* saints. There is another group— even more numerous—to which most of us belong. These can be classed together, in spite of all divergences of expression and degrees (minus degrees!) of sanctity, as the *awkward* saints!

To live with saints in heaven,
Is bliss indeed and glory;
To live with saints on earth
Is quite another story.

How rich the world is in *awkward* saints—rich in the numerical sense, I mean. Take away the awkward saints from Christendom and how many would be left?

Now comes the burning question: *is the awkward saint a finished product*? Has God got him (or her) as far as He possibly can along the way of holiness? Has he (or she) stiffened faultily in the mould, been marred in the making? Are awkward saints the rejects, the chipped, cracked, flawed 'seconds'; the unsuccessful experiments, the imperfect best that the divine Craftsman could produce with such poor quality material? Is there no hope of improvement after 10, 20, 30 years of stagnation?

Firstly, who are we to judge another's spiritual condition? Who but God knows the secret underpull of strong hereditary currents? Who but God can assess the strength of temptation against an inherent weakness of character? Who but He can judge the effort made before open defeat becomes apparent?

We know:
The little catty, criticizing ways,
The gauche self-consciousness she cannot hide,
The grudging, niggard praise;
But God knows:
The soul that sometimes seeks Him in the night
And weeps slow tears upon His heart like rain,
And longs and prays and vows to do the right,
Yet fails, and fails again.

Secondly, who are we to limit the power of God? We believe that God can save sinners from the uttermost to the uttermost. Cannot our faith stretch out to believe that He can so sweep into our lives that sins of the disposition are not only forgiven but conquered; so that awkward saints become *real* saints? Frederick Coutts provides a succinct and positive declaration: 'God is as able to deal with the crooked natures of His perverse saints as with the unregenerate heart of the sinner.' Do we believe that?

Do we believe it for the squabblers, the self-engrossed, the triers of our patience? Have we faith that God can change *them*, straightening out the kinks in their natures, filling out the lacks, reducing the bumps of egotism and pride, smoothing down the prickles? We *must* believe it. If not, we are limiting God's power and our lack of faith is damming up the streams of His grace.

Then I come to my last question, and I put it very tenderly and intimately to you, as I put it to my own heart.

Do we believe that God can change *us*? Have *we* got as far as we shall ever get towards the heavenly uplands? Must we always carry this overwhelming sense of coming short? Or is that just God tugging at us, urging us higher, stabbing us awake and prodding us on? Can it be that we are suffering the *growing pains* of sainthood?

O tell us, those who are the real saints! Those who walk the highways, open your hearts to us. Are the upward paths too rugged for our faltering feet? Are there slopes too steep for us to attempt to climb? Are the footholds too precarious? Can God keep *our* feet from stumbling up there?

'Yes, yes', they call down from the heights. 'He did it for us, He can do it for you. Courage!'

Are we growing spiritually?

WHEN I was a cadet in the Clapton training college in London, we had an old-fashioned officer on the staff who bore that ancient, honourable but now happily defunct rank of Commandant.

One of her duties was to interview us cadets. By the grapevine system of communication used in training colleges, throughout the world, the opening gambit of her interview was known. So when I was called to her office I knew what to expect. It was exactly as I had anticipated.

She stood by the window of her room holding a pot-plant in her hand. Turning to me she said—as I had been warned she would do—'I like *growing* things. Cadet, are *you* growing spiritually?'

That was indeed the very question I had been told would be forthcoming. I had prepared a few answers but they were of the flippant kind and not of the type one could give a training officer, so I murmured a weak, 'I don't know. . . .' It gave her the opportunity she needed.

I was not sufficiently experienced or mature to remind her that growth in holiness is a most tantalizing kind of development. The more you know of God, the worse you see yourself to be. The nearer the light you come, the more the stains on your garments show. The less you sin, the more sensitive becomes your conscience.

And the worst of it is—and the best of it is—that God won't let go! When He has got a man or a woman, He holds on to them. He intends to make something of them. He prunes, He disciplines, He polishes, He refines . . . until one is tempted to cry out: 'Enough! Stay Thy hand.' It is a long and sometimes a painful process. It is simple enough to look good, sound good and at times to feel good, without *being* good.

I used to think that a full consecration, an entire giving of oneself to God, would at once take the spiritual conflict out of a person's life. I don't think so now. God is always showing us new standards of conduct that we should achieve, giving us new revelations of His will, revealing new avenues of service.

There is an attractive advertisement offering *sun-tan in six hours without sun.* We spray it on at night when going to bed and we wake next morning beautifully tanned all over. It may be possible to produce sun-tan without sun, but we can't produce godliness without God. The beauty of holiness is not a skin-food. It is for internal use and only God can apply it.

I come back to the question the old Commandant asked me: 'Are you growing spiritually?'

If I had to answer that today I think I should say: 'I hope so', and as a reason for my hope I would give the following signs: The Bible is alive for me. Texts light up with special reference to my circumstances and become *mine,* a lamp to my feet. My spiritual hunger is keen and prayer has become a habit with me, so that I lift my heart at all times of the day on all kinds of matters, as well as having my set times for devotions. Best of all, God has become greater for me and I long to know that experience of which Paul wrote: to 'be filled with all the fulness of God' (Ephesians 3:19).

Wanted—spiritual cosmonauts
WE live in thrilling days. Nothing seems impossible in the space age. Scientists prepare one great surprise after another for us.

Surely this marvellous age of expansion calls Christians to greater exploits in God's name and power.

The challenge of this age demands that we set about some spiritual discoveries. Christianity today requires spiritual cosmonauts, spiritual research workers and explorers.

How is it that men can live today for months in a space laboratory 'up above the world so high' yet come down to earth again at a given point? Behind this fantastic adventure lie years of dreaming and planning. A few men believed it could be accomplished. Folk laughed at them, reminded them of the law of gravitation, called them fools.

But these scientists dreamed on, dreamed and worked, experimented, died—many of them—but left behind the heritage of this tempting fantasy. Each generation carried the plans further forward, kept alive the hope of final victory, learned how to cooperate with the laws of nature, which are the laws of God.

In the same way spiritual cosmonauts must proceed if they are to explore 'the breadth and length and depth and height' of Christ's love and power.

In what direction shall we look for new discoveries in spiritual realms? I will name some lines which we have already explored to some extent but along which we must go much further.

The first is *the energy of prayer.* Prayer is more than a conversation between us and God. Prayer releases invisible energies which are world-wide in their influence. Prayer helps us personally. Our viewpoint, our reactions, our physical health, even our facial expression, are all affected and improved when we are praying people. But we are only on the fringe of what can be accomplished by the energy of prayer. Further research is needed, experimental research.

Then there is *love's radiation.* Love is more than emotion or sentiment. Love is a radiation of personality from one to another. Even social workers who are not Christians insist on the necessity of caring love for the one to be helped.

While awaiting my turn at a dentist's in Paris, I picked up a magazine and read an article by a French doctor in charge of a clinic for sick babies. He found that babies under his care did not develop as quickly as those looked after by their mothers at home. He investigated and found that to save time the nurses held feeding bottles to two babies at once, standing between the cots. This he forbade, ordering the nurses to take each baby up in their arms at feeding times. Each child in addition must have a half-hour daily in a nurse's arms, during which she would croon and talk and sing to it as a mother would do. The results of the new system fully justified it. Even tiny babies need the radiation of personal love. We who care for the souls of men must learn this lesson anew.

The third subject I would suggest for further research is *spiritual healing,* new health and vigour through faith in God and the consciousness of being in His care. I know that in many lands Christians are following down this avenue of investigation. Faith and prayer can help our physical weaknesses. Many of us have already proved this for ourselves. More exploration is called for.

Lastly, I will name *faith force.* Faith is the contact point between the human and the divine. Faith is the end of our resources and the beginning of God's. How many times did Jesus wonder over the disciples' small faith? And what about us? We must cast off all doubt, all reserve. God's power is at our disposal for spiritual purposes as well as for scientific ends. We must learn to co-operate with God's laws and then we must go forward.

We cannot leave all initiative, all research, all patient tackling of difficult problems, to the children of this world for temporal purposes. We are born of the Spirit for eternity. Let us rise to our inheritance. Spiritual cosmonauts are needed. Will we be among them?

Believe and receive

CAN the gospel be so simple, Lord?
      Believe and receive!
It certainly sounds too good to be true.
Looking along the lines of theological books
      on library shelves
Gives one a frightening feeling of the complexity
      of religion;
Counting the various denominations comprising
      the Christian church
Bewilders the mind.

Your message when on earth, Master, was always
      brief and plain:
Believe and receive, rise and follow, go and tell.
Are these basics sufficient today, Lord?
      Surely they are!

The start on the Christian pathway
      is deceptively simple.
A turning about, a change of direction,
      a freedom through forgiveness,
A new loyalty to a higher Power,
      and then? . . .
A new life, leading into unsuspected paths
      of service
      and adventure for God;
New strength direct from You, Lord,
A source of joy and peace within,
      Your own gift.
Thank You, Master.

23

Home-made bread

WHAT a delightful and tantalizing odour fills a house where new-baked bread has just been lifted from the oven! Fortunately, the art of making bread at home is on the increase, despite the stocks of sliced and packaged varieties on the supermarket shelves. My consumption of bread is so small that it is hardly worth my while to make my own, yet aromatic memories of early attempts, when I had the family around me, float from time to time around the kitchen corners of my brain and tempt me to try again. I call to mind the relaxing and pleasant feeling of seeing the dough rising slowly in a warm place, to push gently upward against the covering cloth.

Then followed the pummelling session, always a bit cruel I felt, when you rewarded the risen dough for its manifest efforts on your behalf by knocking it back to square one, from which it had to start all over again.

But the result! Fragrant, crusty loaves, beautiful to look at and delicately nutty to the taste. No relation at all to the sliced padding masquerading as the staff of life in many shops.

One day, forsaking my old and tried recipes, I fell to the temptation of trying a 'foolproof, no-kneading recipe, as easy as mixing a Yorkshire pudding'. I thought I discerned a snag in it as the amount of liquid advised seemed in excess compared with the amount of flour. Then there was the mystic comment that the dough should be slippery but not wet. My mind tried to conjure up pictures of things that were slippery though not wet, but the only lasting impression was that of a rubber diving suit, hardly applicable to a bread-dough image. A further instruction said that the dough should be mixed with one hand only, which raised suspicions in my mind later confirmed by events.

I collected all the ingredients in a very large bowl as recommended, added the liquid and plunged my right hand in. The result was a fearful mess like thick warm porridge. Getting nowhere with one hand I introduced the other as well, so that both my hands were engulfed in warm wet stickiness. Then the inevitable happened! The telephone bell rang. Quickly scraping the mess from my hands under a running tap and seizing a towel, I answered the phone. Wrong number! Back in the kitchen I again attacked the mess of potage, but all the mixing I did failed to produce anything like dough, slippery but not wet. Mine was definitely wet, horribly wet, and not in the least slippery.

Being of an orderly mind I had put the flour bag in the cupboard after measuring the required amount. Now with cloggy hands I had to open the cupboard door, get the bag of flour and pour from it. When I had used up all the flour in the bag the mixture was still wet!

However, having come so far in my experiment, I was not going to waste the result. I slapped it into two bread tins and could feel it pushing upward against my hand as I tried to flatten it. In a warm place it rose over the edges of the tins, bulged out and started to drip down the sides. I rushed it to the oven, wiped off the drips and closed the oven door. What I got out of the oven a half-hour later was surprisingly edible but very porous, so I don't think I'll try taking short cuts again.

I have lived in several different European lands, each with bread specialities of its own, and learnt to appreciate them all. There is the hard rye bread of Sweden which we know as Ryvita and the wafer-thin flat bread of Norway, the Danish dark rye bread made with malt, without which all Danes languish, and the delicious French bread, metre-long, exceptionally good when freshly baked but not so nice afterwards.

Do we realize how fortunate we are to have so many bread shops around us? Supposing we had to bake all our own bread, after first grinding the corn as they had to do in former days! Usually two heavy round stones were used for the grinding. The top one had a hole in it, through which an upright stick was passed by which it could be turned. It was heavy work, so usually two women helped each other, sitting opposite on the ground outdoors, each with one hand on the stick.

We buy not only flour but also yeast. What should we do if we had neither yeast nor baking powder? We should have to keep our own supply of yeast in the house. When we first set up housekeeping we should ask a neighbour for a little of her yeast, which was a piece of dough from a previous baking to which extra salt was added, then it was set aside for a day or two to ferment. And from that first gift of yeast we should be expected to be self-sufficient for the rest of our days.

I am reminded of a military bakehouse near where we lived in Stockholm, Sweden. Every day thousands of loaves were made for the different regiments, some of the dough being set aside from each baking to ferment and act as yeast for the new bread. One day we heard fire-engines racing along the street with a great deal of noise. My young son asked if we could follow them, so I went with him and found the military bakehouse in flames. Most of the large building was destroyed. Next day we read in the papers that although much baking equipment had been burnt, it had been possible to save some of the dough to act as yeast for future bakings, as had been done *for the last 300 years.*

In the First Book of Kings we have a fascinating story of how the prophet Elijah was fed by a poor widow woman in a time of famine:

'As he [the prophet] arrived at the gates of the city he saw a widow gathering sticks; and he asked her for a cup of water. As she was going to get it, he called to her: "Bring me a bite of bread, too." But she said, "I swear by the Lord your God that I haven't a single piece of bread in the house. And I have only a handful of flour left and a little cooking oil in the bottom of the jar. I was just gathering a few sticks to cook this last meal, and then my son and I must die of starvation."

'But Elijah said to her, "Don't be afraid! Go ahead and cook that 'last meal,' but bake me a little loaf of bread first; and afterwards there will still be enough food for you and your son"' (1 Kings 17:10-13, *Living Bible*). And a miracle took place! The widow's flour and oil lasted until abundant rains brought the new harvest, as the prophet had promised.

What insight this gives us of living on the edge of poverty and hunger, with the last handful of meal and a few drops of oil between us and starvation, plus the extra effort of gathering a few sticks to make a small fire on which to bake the flat bread loaves.

95

None of us has to face such penury, however difficult our circumstances.

There is another woman in the New Testament who interests me greatly and yet we know nothing about her. I refer to the mother of the boy who gave his lunch of five barley loaves and two fishes to Jesus to enable Him to feed a great crowd. I have often wondered why she didn't accompany her son to hear the prophet from Nazareth, and yet I am fairly certain that she stayed at home. Had she gone too, she would have carried a lunch-basket for the two of them, instead of sending him off alone. The mother must have longed to hear and see Jesus, yet on this one day when He is in the neighbourhood and almost everybody has gone to see Him, she remains at home.

Why should she not go with her son? Did she have a sick child at home? Was she near her time with a baby? Was her husband ill? She was not a rich woman, this mother, for the little loaves were made of barley and that was the cheapest and commonest kind of grain, despised by rich people because of its coarseness. She must have been like many of us, busy trying to keep the home wheels turning and the children well and happy. She had been married for some years for her boy was quite big, so she had been doing the same duties day after day for a very long time. It can be most frustrating to make the same beds, wash the same saucepans and dust the same furniture year after year. But the very sameness of these tasks gave the feeling of security to the little family, a sense of belonging together in known surroundings.

The lad offered his lunch to Jesus, five small loaves and two dried fishes, but behind the gift lay the work of the mother in the home. She had ground the flour, made fire in the brazier and pressed the little loaves flat in her hands before baking them in the hot ashes. And what a miracle Jesus performed! In the New Testament we read: 'He took the five loaves and two fish . . . and asked God's blessing on the meal, then broke the loaves apart and gave them to the disciples to place before the people. And everyone ate until full! And when the scraps were picked up afterwards, there were twelve basketfuls left over!' (Matthew 14:19, 20, *Living Bible*).

Jesus accepted the offering made to Him although it was nothing wonderful in itself. Perhaps some of the loaves were a bit burnt or a poor shape. When the boy came home and told his mother all about it, she would have said: 'But I've often baked better bread than that! I was in such a hurry. . . .' Yet our Lord took those simple loaves, perhaps imperfect in themselves, and worked a miracle with them.

And in the same way He will take our offerings of love and service, our 'little loaves', and bless and multiply them beyond anything we might imagine to the glory of His name.

God of the open spaces

GOD of the open spaces,
   God of the wind-swept sea,
Lord of the lofty mountains,
   I open my heart to Thee.

God of the flowering meadow,
   Hear now my earnest plea:
Quicken my flagging spirit,
   Let me commune with Thee.

Healer of nature's woundings,
   Clothing in mantle green,
Heal Thou my spirit's bruises,
   Fill me with joy serene.

Sunrise and sunset praise Thee,
   Raindrop and starry night;
Out of my heart's contentment
   Paeans of praise unite.

Master of all creation,
   E'en though supreme Thou art,
Graciously deign to hear me,
   Live Thou within my heart.

24

Is peace possible?

PEACE is a beautiful word, expressive of its meaning in its sound. And peace is what the world needs today; peace among nations, a world peace that will ensure the best living standards possible for the increasing population. But also peace between the many differing factions within any nation. There is little one ordinary person can do to promote universal peace, but we can each endeavour to create and maintain friendly relationships within our own circle.

It is not only in our time that world peace seems to be an elusive quality. I was very interested to read an account of how the Pope tried to stop European wars in the Middle Ages. In 1036 Europe was full of bloodshed, one feudal baron fighting against another. There was terrible loss of life in the hand-to-hand conflict of that era, and the untilled fields, neglected when the peasants were drafted to fight, resulted in famine. The Pope issued an edict forbidding all private wars, calling his plan 'God's Peace'.

After a brief lull wars broke out again, and were soon in full swing. The Church stood helpless. Five years later the Pope tried again. Realizing that the war lust was too strong to be denied existence, he proposed a compromise. He announced it in a very ingenious document called 'God's Armistice'. Needless to say he had the interests of religion at heart and wanted his people at church on Sundays.

'God's Armistice' forbade all war between sundown on Thursday to sunrise on Monday. Human nature being what it is, the only result of the Pope's edict was that the war warriors rested and fed over the long week-end to throw themselves with renewed ardour into their bloody fights the remaining days of the week. The edict was not long obeyed! The wars continued.

There are various kinds of peace. There is the peace of a cemetery, the peace of death. Whatever differences the people lying there had in life, they are now over. Death is a great equalizer. To walk through a well-kept cemetery is far from being an unpleasant experience. It is a useful reminder that our days are only lent to us for a time, but it is also uplifting for the spirit for all who believe that the soul lives on after the tired body has been laid to rest.

There is the peace of oblivion under an anaesthetic or a drug. That is brief and is followed by results not usually agreeable. In the last few years a number of pop and rock stars, several still in their 20s, have died as a result of an overdose of drugs. With the excitement of standing before an audience night after night, becoming known and hero-worshipped, they have depended more and more on pep pills to keep them going at top potential, then sedatives to slow them down for sleep, plus more insidious drugs to give them their 'highs'.

There is the rural peace of the countryside where the only visible movement is in the throat of a reclining cow chewing the cud. There is a strange phenomenon with absolute quiet. You can hear it! So seldom do our human ears fail to register sounds around us that when there is nothing to notice they become alerted, almost alarmed. There is something awe-inspiring in total silence.

Stillness as I felt it on the top of Mount Beautiful in Lapland was unforgettable. There was space all around as far as the eye could see. Nearby were wooded dales and in the distance smooth rock fells, worn placid by innumerable glaciers in times long past. No hum of insects, no stir of wind. Further down the slopes, but too far for sound to carry, grazed some reindeer, their widespread antlers traced against the sky. Stealthy movement without sound caught my eye. A mother deer, followed by her calf, trotted out of sight.

My heart's laboured thumping after the ascent slowed down. Peace and quiet flooded the nervous system and tension relaxed. A time like that is a moment for communion, when man is infinitely small and God is great—great and powerful, yet loving. The world's harsh music and hectic hurrying seem nightmare dreams that never again will intrude. Here is reality. Here one must face oneself—and God!

There is the peace of untrodden snow in a field. Gone are the varying colours of grasses and weeds, gone too the irregularities of growth and bare patches. All is covered; even, smoothed under a pure white mantle, which hopefully can last a day or two.

There is also the temporary peace of an empty house, possibly with all artefacts of living amply provided, only awaiting the turn of the key in the door when the family returns from holiday. Then peace is abruptly and happily shattered.

But what we need is inward peace, peace of heart. Not the effect of tranquillizers which put a protective fence between us and our worries. Our problems will still be there, but we won't feel them. We will float in a sea of peace and goodwill to everyone and everything for a few hours. Until the drug wears off. This is an artificial solution to stress, right to take on medical advice for a period, but not to be used as an escape from the ordinary wear and tear of daily life.

We live in an age of tension. From the hoardings in the streets by day and by brilliant neon lights at night, we are urged to buy this . . . eat that . . . drink something else . . . use only this product. . . . At home the latest news bulletins bring the whole world's troubles into our living-room, and when we have turned off our television to go to bed we are likely to hear noise from the neighbours through the wall or ceiling. Our minds, our nerves, are bombarded with sensations all the time.

The peace of heart that we need can come only from one source and that is divine. Jesus Christ spoke some lovely words about peace during His ministry on earth: 'Peace is my parting gift to you, my own peace, such as the world cannot give. Set your troubled hearts at rest, and banish your fears' (John 14:27, *NEB*).

God's peace is not like chemical serenity. The effects of it do not wear off after a few hours but rather increase with time. God's peace cannot be bought, however much we might be willing to pay for it. It is a gift and has to be received gratis.

What kind of peace was it that Jesus offered to His followers and that is available to us today? It is not the absence of problems and trials; it is something greater than that. It is peace of heart *in spite of* difficulties, in spite of set-backs, in spite of ill health. God's peace is a triumph of divine grace over human nature. It is not only a Sunday peace but a workaday peace.

If I were asked to name the three main causes of lack of peace in the human heart I should say they were fears for the future, resentments against others and a guilty conscience.

Fears and anxiety for the future are an everyday part of living, for none of us can be certain of what will happen. We can prepare as well as possible for various eventualities, but often the unknown contains a big question mark. The secret of maintaining inward tranquillity is to live a day at a time, committing each new day as it begins into God's hand and refusing to try to see over the wall of the coming months. There seems to be a growing interest in the daily horoscopes published in many newspapers and magazines, where according to your birth date you are encouraged in a certain course of action, or warned against the dire consequences should you follow it. What a farcical way of trying to face up to daily living! God is the only one who knows our future and He sees fit to veil it from us. However, by committing each new day to Him as it dawns, we can count on His guidance and help.

It has been proved again and again that a feeling of resentment or hatred against someone else causes illness. We can have no inward peace while we nourish ill will against those who have wronged us, or we imagine have wronged us, or against those who have a nicer home, a better job or a bigger car. Such feelings act like a poison in our system.

A guilty conscience is an unpleasant companion which will accuse us in harsh terms in the silences of the night or at other moments when we are alone. We are moral beings with a sense of right and wrong, and before the bar of conscience we often stand condemned. Before God we are all guilty, but in His loving mercy He has provided a way of release, of forgiveness, through the sacrifice of His Son Jesus Christ on the Cross of Calvary. Let us listen to those wonderful words which Paul wrote to the Romans: 'Therefore being justified by faith, we have peace with God through our Lord Jesus Christ' (Romans 5:1).

What a sublime truth! Christ took our sins upon Himself, and through Him we have forgiveness and the past can be blotted out. Then, justified by faith, *we have peace with God.* True peace, inward peace. No outward storms can shake it, no hurricane winds can sweep it away. It is the gift of God. For each of us.

25

Mottoes

I LIKE mottoes. I like them in general and I like them in particular. I like them humorous in the style of: 'Always be sincere, whether you mean it or not', and I like them brief and hard-hitting, as 'Do it now!'

Many people adorn their walls and their desks with a variety of these snap phrases, but I am all for a semi-secret unemblazoned motto which can be a lode star for life: something which expresses one's innermost thoughts and aspirations and which helps to hold one true to a chosen course. Such a motto I adopted when I entered the training college in 1926. Its wording originated with Dr Grenfell of Labrador, whose work I admired so greatly. It was: 'To follow Christ is the greatest adventure in life.'

Now when my active service is behind me, I have changed my motto so as to express the inward longing of my heart for the years that remain. After long reflection I formulated it like this: 'To know Christ better: to make Him better known.' Under that banner I hope to serve Him for the rest of my days.

Having reached ripe age without any special physical disability I was taken aback when acute arthritis developed in one of my knees. I had taken it for granted that I could move as freely in age as in youth, so I was quite unprepared for the difficulties a painful knee-cap can occasion.

Deciding to work out a philosophy of action to help make the best of a bad situation, I coined the phrase: 'Good up . . . bad down.' This I repeated hastily as I approached a step, reminding myself to use the best leg first when going up and the painful leg first when going down. My temporary disability was soon over, but it occurred to me that 'Good up . . . bad down' could be a splendid motto for more than one area in life.

God who counts the stars

THE God who counts the starry clusters
   And knows how all the planets turn,
He watches from His highest heaven
   And makes our welfare His concern;
So step by step in perfect love
He guides us to His home above.

In His almighty hands residing
   Lie all the worlds that He has made,
Yet to each single earth-bound mortal
   He sends His Holy Spirit's aid;
And if in childlike trust we rest,
We see His plan is always best.

As all the stars display their brilliance,
   Each in its orbit ne'er to cease,
E'en to my heart the Lord dispenses
   A measure of His light and peace.
Ablaze with stars God's palace stands
Yet me He greets with outstretched hands.

The stars, they shine in destined patterns
   And from their pathways never stray;
So also I am in God's purpose
   And all is well if I obey.
Take, Lord, my hand and shepherd me
Along the path that leads to Thee.

Danish text: Emil Larsen
Translation: F. L.

26

High days and holy days

CHRISTMAS
The coming of a Babe

THE other day when I came home I found a book lying on the sofa which my daughter had taken from the bookshelf. The sight of it brought back memories of my childhood when my father used to read to us in the evenings. One of the stories from that book I remember very well. It was called *The Luck of Roaring Camp,* by Bret Harte.

It concerned a rough gold-mining camp in North America; a camp of wild and uncouth men, some of them fugitives from justice. Only one woman lived in the camp and she was there for no good purpose. Most of the men, bad as they were themselves, despised her. She was of Indian blood and was about to bear a child.

That was a new experience for the mining camp. Deaths were plentiful there, but a birth had never happened previously in anyone's memory. A knot of men had gathered round the old shack where the woman lay when there came the thin, wailing cry of a new-born. One of the older miners was deputed to go in to help the mother but he came out a few minutes later to say that the Indian woman had died and that they were left with an infant boy on their hands.

A collection was immediately taken up for the expenses of the orphan, a miner was chosen as nursemaid, and a she-ass was found to provide milk. The baby was given the name Luck, as they hoped he would bring them luck in their gold-seeking.

The new arrival brought the camp more than luck. The miner-nurse washed his own hands and face and insisted that all who wanted to see the baby must do the same. Such an amount of washing had not been known before in the camp.

A small piece of broken mirror was hung up in the local bar and the rough men smoothed their hair before going to see 'the Luck'. Shirts were washed far more often. As the baby grew the men brought it pretty stones and flowers which they found as they prospected, things that they had never looked at before. Swearing was now frowned upon, as it was not thought proper that the child should hear such language.

In fact, that frail little baby wrought an unbelievable change in the whole mining community. Huts were cleaned up, flowering plants were coaxed up the doorposts. Roads were smoothed for the little feet, gardens were planted. All because of the coming of a babe.

We celebrate the coming of another Child at this season of the year, a Child who has changed the world for many of us. This Child, Jesus, calls out the best that is in us. For His sake we would live better lives; for His sake we try to help others. The little Indian baby in my story was given the name of Luck. The Child whose coming we now celebrate bore a chosen name, a prophetic name, the name of Jesus meaning Saviour: 'For He shall save His people from their sins'.

That is the biggest change that can be brought about in our lives, for it is an inward change in the realm of the soul, the spirit. It is turning from darkness to light; it is being born again of the Spirit of God. This change in our heart will bring about outward changes in our way of life, our thinking, in our reactions and our choices. Our life will be happier because of the coming of the Babe of Bethlehem.

GOOD FRIDAY
The festooned cross

GREY was the day and grey the scene. Coloured with that all-pervading greyness peculiar to Brittany in France. Not a depressing colour but a soothing, hushed and placid grey. Grey-bricked narrow houses with slated roofs, huddled close to each other on both sides of the cobbled streets that led inevitably downward to the bay.

Most of the menfolk were away at their fishing but a few elderly women were about. Clad in black, they added a sombre touch only relieved by the stiffly starched white lace caps perched high on their heads in customary Breton fashion. Dignified they were and quiet, going about their business with serious mien. In the distance the sea shimmered softly, balancing small fishing boats on its swell and then losing itself in a white mist that blurred all distinction between water and sky.

I left the cobbled streets and took the headland path. There under the wide span of the clouded sky stood a crucifix, a typical French wayside crucifix, its wooden foot embedded in a heap of large stones. The cross was so high that I had to strain my neck to look upwards at the figure that hung on it. The head of the crucified Christ twisted sideways, agony visible in His drawn features and half-closed eyes. The sculptor had been lavish in his portrayal of blood from the wounds in hands, feet and side. Red drops exuded where the thorn crown pressed into the Saviour's brow.

Before the crucifix I stood for a few minutes in reverent contemplation, then I turned away towards the cliffs.

I had not gone far when a coach-load of tourists passed in very hilarious mood, singing and shouting. As the coach slowed down at the crossroads where the crucifix stood, some of the holiday-makers, worse for drink, threw paper streamers round it, festooning it with multi-coloured bands. Others in the party began to protest and begged the driver to stop. He drew up as soon as he could and the protesters ran back. One of them tried to climb the cross but it was too high, and the wind blew most of the streamers out of his reach. They had to leave the cross like that for the breeze to strip it of its gaudy trimmings.

I felt sad at heart as I saw it. There was only one thing I could say, and in my heart I said it: 'Father, forgive them, for they know not what they do.' It was an echo of what my Saviour cried from His Cross nearly 2,000 years ago.

EASTER
Remember!

NOW remember! How often we heard those words as children. Remember to say thank you, to wipe your shoes on the doormat, to do your homework . . . remember this . . . remember that. . . . There was no end to it. Why is it that we remember some things and forget others? It is because what interests us fastens better in the mind. We forget what we want to forget!

In Paul's letters to the young Timothy he finds it necessary to remind him of various things. Most of all he urges him to: 'Remember Jesus Christ, risen from the dead' (2 Timothy 2:8, *NEB*). Paul admonished Timothy to think of Jesus Christ, not hanging on the cross but raised by God to life, the resurrected Christ. The conqueror of death!

This is the central point of our faith—that we have a resurrected Saviour. Christianity has no grave of its Founder to which pilgrimages can be made. We worship the Lord of life, risen from the tomb.

Mary of Magdala would always remember that morning. How she stole to the garden in the darkened hush of early dawn to see again the place where her beloved Lord had been laid after the Crucifixion. How she found a dark gaping hole at the entrance to the tomb cut in the rock, the heavy stone having been rolled away. Someone must have stolen the body of Jesus! She ran to the disciples and told them, then love drew her back to the scene. Peering again into the tomb she saw two angels who asked her why she was crying. 'They have taken my Lord away, and I do not know where they have laid him' (John 20:13, *NEB*).

As she turned away she saw someone standing nearby, whom she took to be the gardener and asked if he had taken the body away. A voice replied: 'Mary!' That voice! It was *His* voice! Jesus was alive! In tremulous joy she stretched out her hands to Him, with the one word, 'Master!' Yes, Mary would always remember Jesus Christ, risen from the dead.

There is a Spanish legend of a boy who went to church on Easter Sunday morning to hear the priest say with tears that it had just been reported that Christ's grave had been found, with a well-preserved body showing the nail holes in the hands and the mark of the spear in the side. The priest wept as he announced that there was no longer any ground for the Christian belief in a risen Saviour. People looked in shock at each other and in small sad groups went home until only the boy was left. Then he suddenly woke up to find himself in a crowded church with the choir singing 'Hallelujah! Christ is risen . . .'. It had been an unpleasant dream. Reality remained. Christ lives!

'Remember Jesus Christ, risen from the dead.'

HARVEST
A packet of seeds

IT all began so innocently. From my daughter I received for my birthday one of those large humorous cards now so popular. On the front was the picture of a beautiful bouquet of mixed flowers with the words: 'Knowing that you are one of those people who can see the great in the small, I send you these.' When I opened the card I found a packet of seeds with no label, no picture and no directions.

However, I decided that those seeds should have the very best possible treatment, so I went straight out and bought a large bag of guaranteed first-class germ-free earth for a veranda box. Then in glad anticipation I planted my birthday seeds.

Weeks passed and I was mystified by the looks of the budding plants. They were growing, certainly, but what were they? They were nothing I could recognize. 'All the better,' I said to myself, 'it will be a surprise later on.' It was!

I gave my daughter a good report of the growing seedlings, but admitted that I could not yet tell what they were. She replied rather pessimistically that perhaps they were not flower seeds at all. She was right!

They were the commonest, dullest weeds you can imagine, the sort that grow on any waste-land and try to creep into your garden when you are not watching. And I had grown them in my expensive compost!

I had to laugh and so did my daughter when I told her. She had no idea of what was in the packet when she bought the card. The incident made me remember a well-known text that is rarely preached on. A rather frightening text: 'Whatsoever a man soweth, that shall he also reap' (Galatians 6:7).

It matters not one bit what you *think* you sow, or *hope* you have sown, or *intend* to sow; it is what you *have sown* that you will reap. The picture of a wonderful bunch of flowers on my birthday card led me astray. It is like many of the world's allurements which look so enticing, so satisfying, and yet which can never fulfil the promises made by them.

Sowing seeds! We are all doing it every day. Seeds of actions, words, thoughts. And what we sow we shall one day reap.

27

My grandmother

I REMEMBER my grandmother as a stately and benign figure with an abundance of white hair. Visiting her was always an event and I loved her, although my love was restrained by a certain awe and respect.

Widowed at 29 years of age, Mrs Emily Benwell was left well provided for, so she could continue to enjoy her round of pleasures while leaving the care of the home and children to servants. Tiring of her empty life after a while, she booked into a hotel in London for a last whirl of amusements before taking her own life, which she felt she could do with a clear conscience seeing her children's future was secure. One evening, when returning to the hotel after a dance, she heard strains of singing coming from a railway arch in Bethnal Green. The arch had been turned into a meeting hall and the door-keeper invited her in.

The service was conducted by George Scott Railton and the gospel he gave was hot. An overwhelming sense of futility and sinfulness came over the young widow and she knelt at the Penitent-form in company with some ragged East-Enders. That act of total surrender to Christ completely changed her life.

In Shoeburyness my grandmother started parlour meetings, inviting the poor folk from the nearby brickfields to attend. One night a Mr Taylor told of his conversion, how, when he was dying of typhoid fever, Mrs Benwell watched by his bedside all one night. Three times she had seen his jaw drop in imminent death. Each time she had made him fight for his life, calling him back in the name of the Lord. He had given his heart to God and he appealed for others to do the same. With the two or three men and women who responded to the appeal was my father, then a lad of 10. He was to give over 50 years' service to God and the Army.

Later my grandmother was given the rank of honorary Major and helped in the Army's social work for women and girls. To the end of her long life she was faithful to her Lord and Saviour.

What counts

NOT the depth of my sin
   But the breadth of His grace,
Not the darkness within
   But the light of His face;
Not my weakness of faith
   But the surge of His power,
This, this is what counts
   As I serve God each hour.

Not my many mistakes
   But His pardoning love,
Not my faltering words
   But His witness above;
Not the times I have failed
   But the strength God can give,
This, this is what counts
   In the life that I live.

Not my dullness of sight
   But His guidance so clear,
Not my slackness in prayer
   But God's voice in my ear;
Not my failure to trust
   But His presence so near,
This, this is what counts
   As I walk with Him here.

28

Grow old with grace

THE word 'grace' is a kindly, dignified expression which I want to use in four ways, for it is one of those adaptable words which fits in obligingly with various meanings.

Firstly, with a capital letter, as a good old-fashioned name. I wonder if any babies of our time are called Grace? Years ago it was very fashionable along with Agnes, Hilda, Edith and a few more. Grace is a high-sounding name and surely demands a lot of its owner. Growing old with Grace includes all other friends whom we have known from childhood; folk who knew us at school, in our first job, when newly married or as first-time mothers. Friendship matures with age and becomes richer because there need be no subterfuges. No use pretending to Grace that we came from a fine family living in a country mansion when she remembers having tea with us in our homely street. No use putting on a posh accent to cover our local dialect when old friends are around. Our defences are down, or rather we need no defences. It is so relaxing, so rewarding, to enjoy the company of old friends.

As the years pass, some friends leave us for the great beyond, and the sense of loss is heavy. The circle of near-and-dear becomes smaller, each one left being all the more appreciated and loved. It is harder, but not impossible, to make new friends when one is old. Home leagues, over-60 clubs and adult education classes give fine opportunities to meet other people. Some, however, do not appreciate large groups but prefer getting together with one or two friends instead.

When old folk meet together youngsters need not believe that all they do is to reminisce about the past and sigh for the 'good old days'. Pensioners have great fun together! In a letter to a daily paper a young woman expressed her amazement at the activity and jollity of two sisters—both over 70—who had come to live in the flat over hers. They seemed to bubble over with fun and laughter and really enjoyed life. So should it be!

Secondly, we must try to grow old with grace in the physical sense. It is not easy to remain slim and supple. We pass through the middle years when the least extra indulgence at the table adds to our weight, making us cumbersome round the hips. Movement is not so easy or so quick as before, so the calories do not get burned up, and there we are, taking two or three numbers larger in clothes. Worse is to come. As we near our allotted 'three score years and 10' we diminish in height and our figure inevitably thickens, so that we lose any suggestion of waistline and become more like a barrel for shape. Am I being too hard? I am only writing from personal experience!

We must fight against this physical rotundity by doing exercises, by keeping active, by walking rather than driving, by gardening or some other semi-energetic pursuit. The average lifespan has now lengthened so much that many will pass serenely through their 80s and be well into their 90s while still living actively. By that age most people have thinned down naturally, so we have something to look forward to!

There is much good fun and heroic common sense in the following anonymous verses:

Thanks, I'm awfully well

There's really nothing the matter with me,
I'm just as healthy as I can be.
True, arthritis stiffens my hands and knees
And when I talk, I talk with a wheeze;
My pulse is weak, my blood is thin,
But I'm awfully well for the shape I'm in.

I've arch supports for my aching feet
Or I wouldn't be able to walk down the street.
Sleep is denied me night after night,
And every morning I look a fright;
My memory's failing, my head's in a spin,
But I'm awfully well for the shape I'm in.

Now the moral of this as the details unfold
Is—for you and me who are getting old—
That it's better to say: 'I'm fine!' with a grin,
Than to let folks know what a shape we're in.

114

Even if our body thickens we must resist all stultifying of the mind. Mentally we must remain alert and this means being interested in all that goes on in our world, taking up some new hobbies, trying out fresh skills, launching out into new adventures, even if in a small way. A doctor has written: 'Old age develops a creative urge and power of its own, of which we have hardly taken notice up to now—a second prime of life—a sort of resurgence of vigour after 70. Aliveness of spirit keeps the body alert and functioning.'

I have a friend, one of my very old friends, who started oil-painting when she neared 60 years of age. She has progressed with such skill that she now regularly exhibits and sells her pictures, mostly of flowers or landscapes for she lives in Devon country, but sometimes she is asked to do special assignments of cottages or gardens dear to their owners.

It is the custom in Finland to give a rocking-chair on a 60th birthday. I have even known it given to a 50-year-old. The gentle exercise with the foot to keep the chair rocking is said to be good for the circulation. I read of a woman of 81 who was given a rocking-chair and she sent it back saying she hadn't time for it as she was too busy. Work is often far better for our health than rest.

While advocating a graceful carriage right up into old age, I am not unmindful of the handicapped friends in our midst, who are never able to 'grow old with grace' physically because of some infirmity. How I admire you! I see you struggling on to buses or sitting in wheelchairs, sometimes gardening slowly and painfully, or with crippled hands knitting lovely patterns. God bless you each one! I remember a one-armed home league secretary in Finland who did intricate and beautiful embroidery. I salute such courage in conquering life's handicaps.

There is an oft-quoted prayer of a mother superior which we should do well to ponder and take to heart:

Lord, Thou knowest better than I know myself that I am growing older, and will some day be old. Keep me from getting talkative, and particularly from the fatal habit of thinking I must say something on every subject and on every occasion. Release me from craving to straighten out everybody's affairs.

Keep my mind free from the recital of endless details. Give me wings to get to the point. I ask for grace enough to listen to the tales of others' pains. Help me to endure them with patience. But seal my lips on my own aches and pains—they are increasing and my love of rehearsing them is becoming stronger as the years go by.

Teach me the glorious lesson that occasionally it is possible that I may be mistaken. Keep me reasonably sweet. I do not want to be a saint—some of them are so hard to live with—but a sour old woman is one of the crowning works of the devil.

Make me thoughtful but not moody; helpful but not bossy. With my vast store of wisdom, it seems a pity not to use it all—but Thou knowest, Lord, that I want a few friends at the end. Amen.

The third use of the word 'grace' is about the saying of a brief prayer before a meal. Someone is asked to 'say grace', eyes are closed, heads bowed, and when the 'Amen' is uttered the meal can begin. It is a custom which is falling into disuse in these days, probably most often through carelessness or hurry, but in other cases through the sheer difficulty of assembling the family at one time in one place. Many feel that the custom is without real worth, being a hangover from stricter Puritan standards, while others defend it as a necessary small moment of gratitude uttered to God for all His goodness. But why only at mealtimes? Ought we not to express our thanks to our Maker at other times of the day too? Yes, of course we should, and many of us say: 'Thank You, Lord' a dozen times a day.

But to return to saying grace. We are thanking God for the food provided and asking Him to bless it to our use. Many are the 'graces' that have evolved over the years; some of them pious, some witty and some learned by rote in childhood and then continued by thoughtless habit. Some groups, and even some families, prefer to sing grace.

Is grace necessary? Should we be less able to digest our food without it? I should doubt that, yet I defend the custom of saying grace as a useful reminder that all good gifts, including food, come from the Father above.

A delicate question arises here. Should we say grace only at main meals and not, say, over a cup of tea or coffee mid-morning? Or before sipping a mug of cocoa at night? Where shall we draw the line of demarcation? The problem—if it is a problem—is complicated by our self-indulgent habits of enjoying both meals and snacks in between. My suggestion is that we say grace at the main meals only, yet try to make that more meaningful than a casual repetition. I like to add a 'Thank You, Lord' at the end of a meal.

I wonder how many remember the old-time 'grace before meat' boxes which The Salvation Army issued to friends to place on the dinner-table, where, hopefully, small financial tokens of gratitude to God were placed. A responsible agent called round each quarter to collect the full boxes and hand out empty ones. The money went to the men's social services. This type of collection is now made with a 'For God's sake care' label.

Finally, we must aim to grow old with grace in a spiritual sense; that rich word 'grace' in religious parlance means the unmerited love and mercy of God freely given to us through Jesus Christ our Lord. Spiritual dimensions enrich our lives. We are not simply bodies. The soul—the spirit—lives on when the body decays, and we enter a new phase of life on another plane. This is God's gracious provision for us. It is not something to be feared but to look forward to with glad anticipation.

To know God—to keep in contact with Him by prayer—gives us a sense of peace, of security, wrapped in the Father's love for the present and the future. Paul often uses the word 'grace' in his epistles: 'I thank him [God] for his grace given to you in Christ Jesus' (1 Corinthians 1:4, *NEB*); 'By grace are ye saved through faith; and that not of yourselves: it is the gift of God' (Ephesians, 2:8 AV). This contact with God, this shining of His grace towards us, keeps us secure in His love right up through old age.

May God grant us the joy and satisfaction of growing old with grace in all its meanings, and now let us receive the benediction with receptive and grateful hearts:

'The grace of our Lord Jesus Christ be with you all. Amen.'